NAZI FUGITIVE

The Incredible True Story of an
SS Colonel Who Helped the CIA
Fight Communist Russia

EUGEN DOLLMANN, SS COLONEL

Foreword by David Talbot

Skyhorse Publishing

Skyhorse Publishing books may be purchased in bulk at special discounts for sales promotion, corporate gifts, fund-raising, or educational purposes. Special editions can also be created to specifications. For details, contact the Special Sales Department, Skyhorse Publishing, 307 West 36th Street, 11th Floor, New York, NY 10018 or info@skyhorsepublishing.com.

Skyhorse® and Skyhorse Publishing® are registered trademarks of Skyhorse Publishing, Inc.®, a Delaware corporation.

Visit our website at www.skyhorsepublishing.com.

10 9 8 7 6 5 4 3 2 1

Library of Congress Cataloging-in-Publication Data is available on file.

Cover design by Rain Saukas
Cover photo by Galerie Bilderwelt/Getty Images

Print ISBN: 978-1-5107-5801-8
Ebook ISBN: 978-1-5107-1597-4

Printed in the United States of America

CONTENTS

Contents

FOREWORD
BY DAVID TALBOT

S COLONEL EUGEN DOLLMANN was not one of the most central figures in Hitler's inner circle, but he certainly was the most dishy. As the Rome-based interpreter who linked together the German-Italian axis during World War II, he had unique access to the Führer and his top henchmen, as well as the decadent milieu surrounding Mussolini. He was not as morally depraved as those he served, but his cynicism made him capable of accommodating himself to their baroque evils. Dollmann was a "self-serving opportunist who prostituted himself to fascism." That was the succinct historical judgment of Holocaust scholar Michael Salter. And yet, precisely because he did not drink fully from Hitler's poisoned chalice, Dollmann was able to observe his masters from a droll distance like the world-weary characters played by George Sanders. This perspective—intimate, but detached—makes his memoirs an utterly fascinating and disturbing reading experience.

Dollmann's companion volumes caused something of a sensation when they were published in Europe under the original titles *Call Me a Coward* (1956) and *The Interpreter* (1967). But they have long been forgotten, until now. With America's descent into its own bizarre nightmare, the discovery of these lost memoirs seems exquisitely well-timed. The inner world of fascist power that Dollmann reveals is both all too human and frighteningly monstrous.

The man who enabled Hitler and Mussolini to communicate with each other was a closeted homosexual, serving a regime that sent thousands of gay men to the gas chambers. This is just one of many ironies that defined Eugen Dollmann. To make things even stranger, Dollmann suggests that Hitler's own fondness for boyish-looking men was a well-known secret in certain German circles during his rise to power.

In one of the most memorable passages of the volumes, Doll-mann recalls his frantic shopping sprees in Rome with Eva Braun, Hitler's companion. "She loved crocodile in every shape and form, and returned to her hotel looking as if she had come back from a trip up the Congo rather than along the Tiber." Dollmann was fond of the sweet and simple Braun, who confided her sad life to him. She confessed to him there was no sexual intimacy between her and the Führer. "He is a saint," she told her shopping companion. "The idea of physical contact would be for him to defile his mission."

Dollmann also writes—with chilling if bemused style—about the antics of the debased Italian royalty and the visiting Nazi dig-nitaries who saw Italy as their playground. His account of a de-bauched, late-night party at a decaying Neapolitan palazzo—enliv-ened by a troupe of performing dwarves and hosted by a duchessa whose twisted smile was the handiwork of a knife-wielding jealous lover—is right out of Fellini. And his chronicle of the evening he spent in a gilded Naples whorehouse with Reinhard Heydrich—the dead-eyed SS general known as "the Hangman" who was one of the masterminds of the Final Solution—is right out of Visconti's *The Damned*. Heydrich, who apparently recoiled at the idea of human touch, preferred to take his pleasure from the two dozen half-na-ked women displayed before him by scattering gold coins across the brothel's marble floor and making the women scramble on all fours to gather them.

As the war drew to its close, Dollmann remained a cunning nav-igator of power, working with a group of wily SS officers to cut a deal with future US intelligence legend Allen Dulles, whose own moral dexterity allowed him to defy FDR's orders and make a sepa-rate peace with Nazi forces in Italy. This unholy pact allowed Doll-mann and a number of other even more culpable war criminals to escape justice at Nuremberg. But for years after the war, Dollmann was forced to scurry this way and that along the notorious Nazi "rat-lines"—the escape routes utilized by fleeing German criminals, of-ten with the help of Western intelligence officials.

Dollmann was a master at the Cold War game, offering his spy services to various and often competing agencies. He even tried to extort Dulles, by then CIA director, as his first memoir headed for publication, unsubtly suggesting that anything in the book the spymaster found embarrassing could be made to disappear if the two men reached an understanding.

Dollmann was shrewd enough to realize it was not wise to keep shaking down men like Dulles, and he got out of the spy game. He tried his hand at selling Nazi memorabilia of dubious authenticity. An ardent movie fan, he also put his translation skills at the service of the Italian film industry, providing the German subtitles for Fellini's *La Dolce Vita*.

You will find no deep moral self-reflection in Dollmann's memoirs. But like many morally compromised men, Dollmann has penetrating insights into the flaws of others.

There was little punishment for his sins. He spent some time confined, fittingly enough, in Cinecitta, the Rome film studio that was briefly turned into a prison after the war, and later at a POW camp on Lake Maggiore that he had the sheer gall (or perhaps sick humor) to compare unfavorably with Dachau, because of the camp's watery pea soup and its rain-soaked tents. "At least in Dachau they had wood huts," he observed.

Dollmann lived to the age of eighty-four, comfortably cocooned in his later years in a sunny garret in a blue-colored residential hotel in Munich, where he was surrounded by photos, books, and memorabilia that recalled his past life. He was perfectly content to live in the past, he told an American visitor one day—after all, he had been begun his career as a European Renaissance historian, until he was kidnapped by history.

At one point, his visitor brought up the recently published Dulles war memoir, in which Dollmann was described as a "slippery customer." Dollmann, whose grasp of English was unsure, asked his guest to explain the meaning of the term and was told that it was someone who was shrewd, cunning, Machiavellian.

The old SS man's face lit up with a smile. "Oh! That is a compliment—for me."

INTRODUCTION

BY FIELD-MARSHAL KESSELRING

EUGEN DOLLMANN is a brilliant personality of high intelligence and great personal charm, a man of great diplomatic abilities and a witty conversationalist who was *persona grata* in Roman society. He was also an S.S. officer.

His personal qualities are well reflected in this book, and he has a humorous and ironical pen which is no respecter of persons, and—as its title indicates—certainly not of his own.

But there is more to his caustic, sparkling book than just wit and brilliance. There is something else, something deeper and more appealing: a reflection of his firm determination to help the Italian people in their misfortune and to blunt as far as possible the hateful excesses inevitable in any fratricidal strife.

I knew Dollmann well, and in these few lines I hope to bring him closer and make him better understood to those who did not know him. There is, I believe, a key to the understanding of his strongly individualistic personality and of the role he played in the events, often fantastic, in which he was involved, and that key is to be found in his upbringing.

He was born in 1900, the son of a Bavarian lawyer. But it was his mother—whose grandfather was Physician in Ordinary to the Empress Elizabeth of Austria, and whose father was legal adviser by appointment to the Court of Bavaria—to whom he primarily owed his introduction to the intellectual and social life of Munich and Vienna, and it was the atmosphere of these two outstanding cities which helped to form his subsequent outlook.

He studied literature and history, and in particular the history of art, at Munich University, taking his degree *"magna cum lauda"* in 1926 with a doctoral thesis on "The Political Ideas of Freiherr Lazarus von Schwendi and the Problems of the Counter-Reformation". Subsequently a financial grant for a number of

xi

years allowed him to pursue an extended course of studies in the great libraries and archives of Italy, and this led to the writing of his historical work on *The Farnese Family*. It also brought him into close contact with leading ecclesiastical and scholarly circles in pre-war Italy and secured for him the great privilege of free access to the Vatican Library and its secret archives.

These valuable connections in Italy (which included the opposition grouped around Benedetto Croce) soon attracted the attention of influential people in Berlin to Dollmann, and from 1937 onwards he worked under the German Ambassadors in Rome, von Mackensen, von Bergen, and the latter's successor von Weizsäcker, serving chiefly—thanks to his fluent command of Italian—as interpreter to German deputations to Italy and Italian deputations to Germany. When Hitler visited Italy in 1938 Dollmann was the interpreter for him and the Duce, and from then on to the end Dollmann was present as interpreter at all Italo-German discussions on both sides of the Alps.

To facilitate the services he rendered during the war to the German Commander-in-Chief in Italy and to the German Ambassador at the Papal Court—particularly in connection with the more and more thorny problem of the relations between the Catholic Church and the Third Reich—Dollmann was given a commission in the ordinary S.S. forces, and he served under General Wolff, the Supreme S.S. Commander in Italy, from the latter's arrival in September 1943 until the capitulation. Incidentally, Dollmann never had anything whatever to do with repressive measures. These were the province of the head of the German Security Service in Italy, Kappler, who was also a subordinate of General Wolff.

In my capacity as Supreme Commander, South-South-West Area, I gladly made full use of Dollmann's services whenever skilled diplomatic intervention was needed to iron out the difficulties which arose from time to time between the army, the Party and the Italian Fascist leaders, and it was at my recommendation that Dollmann was promoted to the rank of full colonel.

Shortly after the defection of Italy Dollmann joined my staff as liaison officer to General Wolff, and during the dramatic period that followed he rendered me very valuable services. But not only me—also the Italian people. In return for the complete confidence I placed in him I demanded absolute frankness, and in this respect he never failed me. And because I knew that I could rely absolutely on h's loyalty he was always able to count on a favourable hearing for his frequent proposals both to humanize the war where possible and to preserve Italy's cultural treasures.

Despite the title of his book, the truth is that he never hesitated to risk his life whenever necessary, and some of the missions he undertook were unquestionably dangerous, for they brought him into contact both with the Italian Partisans and with Italian Fascist formations, some of which bore no enviable reputation.

And when the time came he was just the man—as his success subsequently confirmed—to initiate the discussions which began in the autumn of 1944 through the medium of the Cardinal-Archbishop of Milan with the head of the American Secret Service in Switzerland, Allan Dulles, and untimately resulted in our capitulation.

I can vouch for the accuracy of his fascinating descriptions where the subject is within my knowledge and I feel quite confident that the rest of his book is equally accurate.

And finally, I feel I must stress that Colonel Dollmann was, all in all, very far removed indeed from what the world has come to think of as a typical S.S. officer. To the best of his ability and to the limit of his power he did his utmost to reduce the sufferings of the Italian people—and to some extent he succeeded. His book, which naturally deals only with one aspect of the whole complicated process, is ample proof of this.

ALBERT KESSELRING

Bad Wiessee, April 12th 1955.

Translated from the German
by

EDWARD FITZGERALD

In the Reichs Chancellery, Berlin, *from left to right*: Adolf Hitler, the author, Count Ciano, von Ribbentrop.

In Hitler's Wolfsschanze (wolf's lair), *left to right*: an Italian officer, the author, Gereal Gariboldi, Hitler, General Halder, Field-Marshal Keitel

Chapter I

HOLLYWOOD IN ROME

WE FONDLY imagined that everything was going to stay nice and friendly. Four days previously I had returned from Florence where the final negotiations for our capitulation had taken place. I had negotiated with General Clark, drunk champagne, eaten Californian tinned fruit, strolled around in full uniform in the company of Allied officers, and finally I had been flown back to Bolzano in an American plane. Now I was sitting with General Wolff on the terrace of the Royal Villa enjoying the bright Italian sunshine.

Wolff had the reputation of being a very lucky man. He was lying comfortably in a cane deck-chair and staring idly at the hedge of roses that separated our little island of the blest from the rest of Italy, and in particular from the Italian partisans. He had in fact always been a very lucky man. Once chief of Himmler's personal staff, he had been in Italy now for about eighteen months. Before that he had been liaison officer between Himmler and Hitler. Having fallen into disfavour with Himmler he had been transferred to Italy, a very fortunate fate in the circumstances.

Then the capitulation had come and we had conducted dramatic negotiations during the course of which Wolff had signed or initialled dozens of documents, minutes, agreements and so on. Now he stretched his long legs in his chair and observed:

"It's really rather pleasant here, Eugenio."

At first I made no reply. My thoughts were on the American tanks whose distant rumbling we could hear even through the great park of the villa, and I had a rather uncomfortable feeling in the pit of my stomach.

"I have a feeling that this is going to be your last birthday in sunny Italy, *Herr General*," I said finally.

1

Not that I was at all clear in my mind as to how this business was going to end, but I certainly had a feeling that we were not going to be allowed to stay here indefinitely, undisturbed by the Allies and surrounded by roses, wives and household goods, with at least twenty cars at our disposal and enough petrol to take us at least as far as Portugal. Whatever the future might hold, it seemed unlikely that it would unroll in the Royal Villa at Bolzano complete with pet dogs and roses.

"Oh, I don't know, Dollmann," he replied.

But the fact that he used my surname this time seemed a safe indication that he too judged our situation rather less favourably than he pretended to.

"Of course, they'll take us to Caserta," he went on, "but that needn't be for a long time yet."

Having regard to the menacing sound of arms which reached us even here from the town I did not altogether share his optimism, but I said nothing.

"And they'll treat us fairly decently I think."

Wolff got up from his chair and strolled up and down in front of me. His tall rather stooping figure robbed me of the sun at every few paces, and the constant play of light and shade on my face made me nervous.

"I don't know whether we can be all too sure of that, *Herr General*," I replied.

Wolff stopped in his stride and looked at me. Then he burst out laughing.

"My dear Eugenio! You're not going to get the wind up in these lovely surroundings? And on my birthday too!"

"Not the wind up exactly," I said, though I wasn't so certain even about that. "But I can't help feeling that things are going to get really uncomfortable, even on your birthday."

"What makes you think that?"

"Remember the fortune-teller, *Herr General*."

Personally I remembered her very well. That old oracle of the Appenines really had been like a witch. Long before we had had any thoughts of capitulation I had dragged Wolff up to see her and she had performed like a witch in a fairy story, complete with purring cat on her shoulder, an open fire on the hearth and a pungent stink of garlick in the one room she occupied in a ruined house. She hadn't been very encouraging: hard times were ahead and things were going down hill rapidly.

"It wasn't worth coming all this way to listen to that," Wolff had observed.

I thought it appropriate to remind him of her prophecies now. "But of course they'll take us to Caserta," I concluded quietly.

"Of course," he agreed. "Of course they will. But what about it? A few hearings, an examination or two, and the matter's settled. And further . . ."

I never heard what was to happen after that, because at that moment Wolff's wife, the former Countess Bernstorff, came out of the villa, smiled at us and told us that lunch was ready. The general shrugged his shoulders and followed his tall, blonde wife into the house. Frau Wolff was a rare type. She had blue eyes and she did her hair up in a sort of crown on top of her head. She was friendly but with a certain reserve and she moved with the cool aloof elegance of the German Baltic aristocracy. Altogether she made a striking contrast to the light-hearted southern temperament of the Italian women around us.

Slowly I got up and followed them into the house, whose fascist rococo style turned my stomach over every time it was borne in on me. Wolff's children were playing in the garden and picking flowers, and soldiers were moving casually around amongst the tents pitched on the great lawn—and it suddenly struck me again how grotesque our situation was.

Staff officers of the *Wehrmacht* drove up in full uniform to congratulate the *Herr General* on his birthday, striding around proudly with their medals up, drinking champagne and eating delicacies, chatting in the flower-decorated corridors around the entrance hall, whilst lower mortals in uniform presented arms in a style worthy of the parade ground on the Kaiser's birthday. And it was all taking place in a town controlled by an American *Kommandatur* and full of hundreds of Italian partisans, and in a country that had capitulated ten days previously and was now almost completely occupied by Allied troops. And the house and grounds in which it was all taking place were separated from the American military police patrols by no more than a hedge of roses.

I stood in the hall with Wolff and discussed the situation with him as we had been doing for days. The only difference now was that I had a very uncomfortable feeling that the whole affair was about to be settled without reference to us or our opinions.

"Has it occurred to you that our situation is quite ridiculous, *Herr General*?" I inquired.

The *Herr General* was unwilling to admit it, and in any case, within the next half-hour it was to be fundamentally changed. Our conversation was interrupted by a rumbling noise that grew louder and louder, and the arrival of the tanks put an end to it altogether.

They rolled through the wide gates of the park one after the other and turned towards the house. Looking out of the windows we could see the white helmets of American military police who had hustled our guards away from the gates and were now running towards the house.

"The Americans," said Wolff in an undertone.

It was an observation which required no comment and I made none. The tanks stopped on the lawn and when the military police had surrounded the villa they came running in at the door, shouting and making a great deal of noise. I remember finding time to be astonished at their behaviour after the quiet and peaceful negotiations which had arranged the capitulation. I was to learn not to be astonished at anything they did.

They were already in the hall, the straps of their helmets under their chins in a businesslike fashion and their machine-pistols aimed at us. They had brought the children in out of the garden and they pushed them ahead of them into the hall. The sight of the grim and determined faces of men out to do their duty at all costs robbed us of any inclination to protest. I think that Frau Wolff did open her mouth to complain but the sight of those dull barrels pointing in our direction was enough and she said nothing.

We were petrified and we must have looked it, for the Americans now began to laugh heartily. But they wasted no time: systematically they laid hands on everything of value they could find in the villa and which would go into their pockets or could be carried out and stowed away in their jeeps. One of their officers came up to Wolff and me. He had one hand in his pocket and he addressed us in German. Between the steady champing of his jaws as he masticated his chewing gum he told us to get ready. Wolff looked at him inquiringly.

"You're to get yourselves ready. Put your things in a small case. Go on, get a move on."

We got a move on. There was nothing else to be done. Behind us marched two enormous military policemen—no doubt the terror of all the unfortunate G.I's they came in contact with. And they weren't too gentle with us either. They hustled us off to our rooms, watched us pack our cases and pocketed the things that wouldn't go in—their uniform jackets had very capacious pockets. Then cursing loudly, but at the same time highly amused, they shooed us down the stairs back into the hall and out through the door, where they packed us both into a jeep—"packed" is the right word.

Just as the jeep was about to drive off amidst the jeers of the hilarious Americans my Alsatian, Argos, tore up, obviously intending to attack the driver. I called him to order at once and Argos stood there obediently but whining excitedly. The Americans weren't laughing now and their officer was cursing. They had drawn their pistols and it was obvious that they intended to shoot the dog. As I could see no way of saving the poor beast from an undeserved death at the hands of the enemy but by doing the job myself, I asked the officer if he'd let me. For a moment he seemed dumbfounded, but then he bellowed:

"No! Get the hell out of here!"

And off we drove. I could hear Argos howling. Then there was the sound of a shot, and no more howling. When we came out onto the road there were American soldiers everywhere. Masses of them, on foot and in tanks and jeeps. All of them were bristling with weapons. Machine-guns were in position and storm companies were ready to go into action.

"Any idea what all this is in aid of, *Herr General?*" I asked.

Wolff was sitting silently next to me and I knew that he was thinking of his wife and of what might happen to her. I wanted to take his mind off the disagreeable subject. I pointed to the strong American forces that seemed to have occupied the whole neighbourhood around our villa.

"You don't really think that's all for our benefit, do you, *Herr General?*"

"What else?" he said shortly. But then he began to laugh. And when I saw all those heavily armed G.I.'s fiddling with their weapons—at least a fully equipped Division mobilised for the sole purpose of storming our peaceable rose garden and capturing our two-hundred-man-strong headquarters—it struck me as ridiculous too and I joined in. The American policeman sitting in front of me had to threaten us with his machine-pistol before we stopped.

Partisans were lining the road. They weren't laughing; they were shrieking with rage at us. From that point of view our heavily-armed escort came in useful and we arrived safely, if not happily, at the Bolzano town gaol.

You have to cast your mind back to the Restoration of 1815 architecturally to get any idea of what Bolzano gaol looks like. Under the name of Bozen, Bolzano once belonged to Austria, and the Austrians had built the prison. As composers of waltzes the Austrians have a very light touch, but as prison builders they more than make up for it. It was one of the grimmest and gloomiest dungeons I have ever come across, and that's saying something because although at that time I had not had much experience, in the future I was to have ample opportunity of studying—at leisure and from the inside—no less than thirteen other buildings erected for a similar purpose.

Once inside the prison Wolff and I were separated and taken off through damp and smelly corridors to different cells, each of us escorted by heavily-armed military police. We knew nothing about the fate of Frau Wolff, the children and the other members of his household, or of the few soldiers who were still in the villa when the Americans arrived.

My escort pushed me unceremoniously into a gloomy and altogether uninviting cell. Until late that evening I had plenty of opportunity to review my situation, and in the meantime I sweated in the close heat and longed for a drink. Then a fat G.I., who apparently worked in the kitchen, brought me some sandwiches and a small glass of water. After that, still very thirsty, I fell into a restless sleep.

Wolff and I walked up and down together between the tent lines in Modena camp. Neither of us could sleep. As soon as we dropped off we were woken up again by the mosquitoes that came up from the surrounding marshland intent on sucking human blood. After a while we had given up the struggle against them—there were too many—and now we went up and down, our bodies covered with bites and scratches, between the rows of sleeping prisoners of war.

The day before we had been brought here from Bolzano at top speed. On the market square in Verona our escort had allowed Wolff to say good-bye to his family, which had followed after us in a lorry. Surrounded by howling Italians who spat at us and threw stones, the General said good-bye to his wife and children. I felt gratitude and a new respect for the American Negro, for without those coloured soldiers we should have ended that evening hanging from an Italian olive tree.

After another top-speed journey in jeeps we landed in Modena camp. Modena is a small rococo town surrounded by marshland and infested with mosquitoes. The Americans had pitched a few tents in a field in the middle of this marshland, and that was the camp. There was nothing to eat and drink, but plenty to do. They kept us busy. An American officer would bawl out an order and the men in the camp, mostly German prisoners of war, would get to their feet and then do as they were told. It might be a course of knee bending, or perhaps they would have to undress themselves and dress again at top speed, or lie down on the ground again.

During a pause in all this business Wolff and I strolled up and down together. The prisoners of war lying around took no notice of us.

"The way the Americans are behaving is disgraceful," said Wolff.

I looked at a group of prisoners who were just engaged in undressing again under American orders.

"I wouldn't blame them if they polished us off," I said.

Wolff looked at me suspiciously.

"Who?" he demanded.

"Our fellows."

Wolff looked over the camp. The sky was gradually growing darker and the swarms of mosquitoes were rising again from the marshes.

"Perhaps you're right," he agreed. "After all, we did tell them they'd be treated decently if we capitulated."

At that moment a tall officer of the American military police happened to pass us going towards a group of prisoners who were now undressed and were being made to practise knee bends in their birthday suits to the great delight of swarms of mosquitoes. I stopped the man and declared shortly:

"I want to speak to the commandant."

The officer stopped, looked me and Wolff up and down, said nothing and turned to continue his way.

"I want to speak to the commandant," I repeated boldly, though inside me I was more than half afraid he might shoot me out of hand. Wolff looked pale too, but that was because we hadn't had anything to eat I decided. Then Wolff spoke, and at first I thought it was another example of the gods first driving mad those they intend to destroy.

"You don't seem to realize who we are," he said.

I found that he said it too loudly. The American still stared at us wordlessly as though he were nonplussed, then he turned about and went off smartly to the camp office.

Half-an-hour later we were again in a jeep driving out of the camp stared at by the prisoners of war, some of whom shouted "Swine!" "Criminals!" and so on. I couldn't really blame them. Then we were driven through the narrow streets of Modena accompanied by angry shouts from the Italians, who certainly seemed to realize who we were. Only the broad backs of our Negro escort stood between us and them and although we were safe enough we didn't feel much like knights "*sans peur et sans reproche*".

Our next port of call was a school and there we were welcomed quite politely—not so much by officers of the German Military Intelligence in Italy who were being held there, as by a group of American journalists. The former treated us as though we had the plague and to loud remarks to the effect that they wanted to have nothing to do with us we were pushed out of the room. At this point the Americans seemed to think that they'd have a little fun with General Wolff. They took us away from the hostile German officers and led us along a corridor out into the courtyard. On the way we heard a number of disagreeable remarks on the part of our compatriots who seemed anxious that we should come to a sticky end. One of them observed, loud enough for us to hear: "They'll shoot those two to-night I expect, and a good job too."

It occurred to me that we two had negotiated the capitulation and put our signatures to it and that in consequence these gentlemen were now safely in a position to wish us ill without coming to any harm themselves.

"Our Intelligence friends are ungrateful," observed Wolff with a cynical grin, "but ingratitude is a professional characteristic."

"Very true," I replied, "but what can you expect? That's those gentlemen all over. By all the laws of war some of them have earned the rope. I don't mind them so much; it's the other poor devils. The ordinary fellows in Modena camp for example."

And whilst the Americans hustled us along the corridor and down a narrow flight of steps into the courtyard Wolff said regretfully: "And we promised them so much. . . ."

One or two reporters interrupted him, talking excitedly and laughing they pushed us in front of a gun in the courtyard. Wolff had to stand in front of its muzzle whilst they danced around taking photographs from all angles. No doubt the pictures were to be symbolic. When they had finished with us we were taken away and put into a gloomy wooden cubby hole. Rats were squeaking excitedly and scampering around behind the rotting woodwork.

"Tell me, Eugenio," said Wolff, "don't you think the Intelligence gentlemen are probably right?"

"What do you mean, *Herr General?*" I asked in simulated surprise. I knew perfectly well what he meant, but I let him explain.

"That this will very likely be our last night," he went on. "I have a feeling they're going to shoot us."

And so had I. The business with the photographs in front of the gun had looked very much like our last photograph before the end; a pleasant little souvenir. Inwardly my nerves were on edge and at any moment I expected the door to open on the execution squad, but I wasn't letting Wolff know that.

"I really don't think so, Wolff," I said. "After all, we did sign the capitulation. We prevented a lot of disagreeable things; saved Italy from further destruction. . . ."

And a great deal more in the same strain. In the end I almost convinced myself that as we had done so much for the sake of peace and to stop death and destruction they wouldn't shoot us after all, and I grew calmer and so did Wolff. But as soon as he said that after all he agreed with me, and began to give his reasons for agreeing with me, I found myself doubting my optimism once again, though I didn't admit it. Half an hour later it was the other way round, and the night passed in self-torture of this kind—a night we both inwardly believed would be our last.

It wasn't our last night after all, but it was our last night both in Modena and in the hands of the Americans. The next morning we were taken out of our improvised cell.

"If you want to pray now's the time, Dollmann," said Wolff.

But I didn't want to pray, and in any case I shouldn't have had much time. Our escort was unusually polite, which seemed another indication that we were about to be shot, but they were in a hurry and our "last journey" was taken at the double. We were hustled along the corridor, down the stairs and out into the courtyard where we found a big British army car waiting. To my excited imagination its black paint and chromium metal made it look like a rather large coffin. I supposed that some high officer had arrived to be present at our execution, but I was wrong.

An English officer got out of the car and the Americans saluted him and pushed us carefully towards him. We were still in full uniform and for the first time for quite a while someone greeted us without bawling or spitting at us. The Englishman saluted us as though it were a matter of course and said: "Good morning, gentlemen." Rather hesitantly we returned his greeting. It seemed too good to be true.

"Perhaps we're going to have a last meal with porridge," whispered Wolff.

I didn't find that very funny and I didn't laugh. Neither did Wolff. The Englishman invited us with a wave of his hand to get into his car. We got in and sat down on the upholstered seats. There was no escort this time, only the driver and the English officer. As we drove out of the courtyard the American military police guard presented arms.

"Every man has a right to change his opinion," said Wolff.

And then in our relief we both began to laugh heartily. And whilst the car sped swiftly along the road to Florence we both assured each other that we hadn't really believed that we were going to be shot. Oh, no! But in the meantime we had no idea where our British guardian angel was taking us. Each of us knew that the other was lying, but in our present quite pleasant situation the previous night seemed like a bad dream.

The British officer, a major, was sitting beside the driver and he turned round to us, amiably offering us his packet of cigarettes. We each took a cigarette and accepted a light from him as though it were the most natural thing in the world, though after our experiences with the Americans we were not altogether sure about the behaviour of our capitulation partners.

Shortly before we came to Rome the officer informed us that we should be staying there for a while. Altogether everything now seemed more encouraging, and in any case I had quite expected the British to behave themselves better than a horde of American cowboys stuck into police uniforms. After a while I spoke:

"Now I don't know what you want with us but tell me: don't you think you're likely to get more out of an officer if you treat him decently?"

Wolff looked at me as though I were someone who had just come up and whose absurdities were therefore not to be taken seriously, but the British officer nodded his agreement and he even smiled.

"Yes, of course I do," he said.

His words and his smile consoled me and Wolff too. After that the rest of the journey to Rome passed to the accompaniment of polite conversation about the traditions of civility practised by the various nations.

11

In Rome we saw groups of girls standing on street corners and cadging cigarettes from G.I.'s. The picture was familiar; only the uniforms of the soldiers were different. The year before when Rome was evacuated and I had driven out of the town the girls had been the same but the soldiers had been Germans. The cigarettes were different too. Ours had been in plain cardboard packets, the American packets were wrapped in cellophane. Otherwise very little seemed to have changed.

I asked the Englishman how Roman society was taking the change. He turned round to us.

"I don't know what you think of Roman society," he said.

"Not much," said Wolff, and I nodded my agreement.

"Neither do I," went on the Englishman. "They're too anxious to please."

"So they were with us," I said.

The Englishman's mouth twitched as though he were going to laugh and then he said seriously: "I don't think I've ever known a social group which so prostituted itself."

At that moment we passed a number of women around a couple of Americans who had a cardboard case of tinned food with them and he went on: *"That's* not what I mean. Those women are hungry and you can understand it. But I can't help feeling that 'the upper ten thousand' behave themselves much worse."

"In what way?" asked Wolff.

"Those women are prepared to squabble over a tin of bully beef, but I shouldn't like to tell you the lengths so-called high society will go for a few cigarettes."

As we drove through the streets of Rome the bells of St. Peter's began to sound. It was six o'clock and the unchanging ritual of the Church demanded that evening service should now take place. At that moment I had the feeling that the Catholic Church would outlast everything and that it was quite inconceivable that an evening would ever come when the bells of St. Peter's did not ring for evening service. I asked the friendly officer how the British got on with the representatives of the Church and whether they had changed in any way.

"They never change," he said, and he laughed. Then he grew serious again and I had the impression that he spoke with conviction: "They were the only ones who didn't change and I believe they never will change."

The bells of St. Peter's died away as he finished speaking. The sky was gradually growing red as the sun sank and everything was still. In the distance we saw the shadow of the Forum Romanum and there was no constant sound of planes in the skies as there had been on my last visit. Our car drove out to the Italian film town, the so-called Cine Città, past the dark shapes of ancient Rome, and for the first time the Italian capital seemed worthy of the name "The Eternal City".

Maxl of Auschwitz was our only source of communication. His name wasn't Maxl at all and he didn't come from Auschwitz, but that's what the English called him and as I can't remember his real name now, that will do. Maxl wasn't an S.S. man or even an intelligence officer; he was just a dog, a dachshund that had belonged to General Pohl. He was the only living being that got enough to eat in the hands of the British Intelligence Service at the Cine Città. The rest of us sat in our cells or under canvas in the camp surrounded by barbed wire and Maxl went from one to the other with messages hidden under his collar.

I was again separated from Wolff and I had "Cell No. 100". It was the former dressing room of a film star which had been turned into a cell complete with bars and barbed wire. In it was a field bed, three blankets, a table, a chair and a hand-basin. During the day I had plenty of time to think things over and there was so little to eat that meals didn't take up much time either. I found myself thinking a good deal of the last time I had been in the Cine Città.

As far as I can remember it was in 1938. We were invited to the Cine Città by the German Embassy to watch a film being shot by an Italo-German film company. It was a blood and lust production called "Beatrice Cenci". I could remember drinking champagne in a certain amount of discomfort before the walls of a fake mediaeval castle. In the film a Renaissance noble seduced his sister and then handed her over to his father for further service, after which, having fulfilled her womanly functions, she was brutally murdered. The star of this wretched film was a German actress. I know that she is still alive to-day,

13

but fortunately I can't remember her name. What I could remember then was that she had occupied the dressing-room which was now Cell 100. The thought didn't make my quarters any the more agreeable.

On one of those boring evenings when I was alone and had nothing better to do than remember this and that detail of "Beatrice Cenci", and wonder what news Maxl would bring under his collar on his morning rounds the next day, the cell door opened and an elderly rather stooping gentleman was ushered in. I knew him quite well. He was—or had been— Intelligence chief to Helferich.

"Good evening," he said politely. And as I looked at his typical old Austro-Hungarian aristocrat's face (I think all Austrians begin to look like Franz-Joseph when they get older) and his scraggy neck which disappeared into a much-creased tunic still bearing his decorations, I fully expected him to add: *"Charmant! Charmant!"* But he didn't play his role properly. Instead he sat down rather heavily on the spare bed and began to talk about food. I listened for a while, but then it became quite clear that he was talking to himself. As my mind turned almost mechanically to "Beatrice Cenci" so his turned to past culinary pleasures: spaghetti and Frascati wine.

After that I paid no further attention to him, particularly as he was a type I disliked. He was, I knew, plagued by a wife who devoted all her efforts—in vain—to remaining young. He always gave off an aroma of heather scent and he never appeared without his decorations (chiefly from the Great War). He would bow and click his heels to us and turn on all his Viennese charm—but that was when the Americans were far away in North Africa. With them and their allies on the spot he would gladly have strung us up with his own hands if the victors had allowed him. But primarily his life was filled with food and wine—thoughts of food and wine now. I am perfectly certain that if we could have offered him better food than the British he would have been making up to us once again.

Fortunately they didn't leave him long in my cell, and after a couple of days or so—full of talk of food and wine interspersed with indignation at the crimes of the S.S. (which he seemed just to have heard of)—he was transferred, and once again I

14

could watch the sun set over the distant Neapolitan hills in peace. After that I had a former chief of our Intelligence as a cell-mate for a few days. As soon as Germany collapsed he went over to the British with all the evidence he could lay hands on concerning the support secretly given by Switzerland to the Third Reich in money and materials. Naturally, the victors thought a lot of him and he was soon transferred to a special camp with better food.

My next companion was very much more agreeable. It was Baron von Griesheim, a major in Helferich's Intelligence. He had been the most determined representative of the July 20th plot in Italy and I had always marvelled at the way he managed to keep out of trouble. Now I wondered how on earth the British had come to put him under arrest. He was friendly with the highest Jewish finance aristocracy in Berlin, and a bosom friend of Count Albrecht von Bernstorff. In fact he belonged to the inner anti-Hitler circle in Germany, most of whose members had ended up in concentration camps.

He made a very pleasant change from most of the prisoners at Cine Città, who did nothing but bemoan their fates. Baron von Griesheim never complained—and, of course, there was no deliberately bad treatment in British hands. He didn't even complain of the food, though, heaven knows, there was cause enough for reasonable complaint there! And he never felt sorry for himself. He just chatted agreeably about his past life, which had been very colourful, and if he repeated many of the old jokes current in Roman high society, he told them in a way that almost made them seem fresh. All in all he was most strikingly different from most of the others who were my fellow prisoners in Cine Città.

Most of the Germans in the camp were in the depths of despair. A man known as "the hangman of Paris" was a case in point. There is no need to mention his real name; I'll call him "S". Every night he would cut open his veins at the wrist, using a safety-razor blade which the British provided him with. Although we were prisoners we were all given razors—the British set some store by neatness of appearance. It was said that they had ulterior motives with this generous supply of razor blades, but I don't suppose for one moment it was true. However, S. certainly used his blade, and every night he would be carried out of his cell with his wrists crusted with dried blood, bandaged up and put back again for the following night, when the same wretched performance began again. I don't know whether S. ever succeeded, but he tried often, if not hard enough.

Wolff was with other Generals now and he was allowed to walk up and down with them behind a glass wall. One day a letter arrived for him from his wife, and for some reason or other the Camp Commandant passed it on to him through me. There was something about the light of the moon in it—perhaps because it is one of the rare things writers and recipients of prison letters could share. Anyhow, after that the light of the moon appeared in almost all camp letters and Wolff turned poet, with moonlight as his main subject.

Another prisoner in Cine Città was young Canaris, a nephew of Admiral Canaris, the former chief of German Military Intelligence, who was hanged in Flossenburg just before the collapse. Young Canaris, who had been Intelligence chief in Brussels, had a fixed idea that he was doomed too, and he could see himself in graphic detail, shot dead and lying in his blood. Not satisfied with that, he was very anxious that we should all be quite certain that we were going to share his fate. The poor wretch was not a very agreeable or soothing prison companion at all. As soon as you spotted his long nose and his staring eyes you knew you were in for a new batch of his horrible presentiments. He was really to be pitied, I suppose, but no one had any time to pity anyone else. Everyone was already too sorry for himself. And as for suicide, the British didn't seem to mind much one way or the other. Somehow it made the idea less attractive.

Then there was a former Security Service officer in Rome, a typical subaltern creature who ought really to have been an N.C.O. His only aim in life was to carry out orders, and this he did conscientiously. The only thing was that, having done so, his conscience troubled him, and all the executions he had carried out now haunted him in his dreams, or, rather, nightmares. Every night he would toss and turn on his field-bed, groaning and moaning, and re-experiencing all the terrible things he had done.

For a time young Canaris was in the same cell with him. They must have been a bright pair. In the end neither of them could stand it any longer, and Canaris asked to be transferred to the open camp to escape from the nightmare executions of his cell companion.

We had Italian prisoners with us too, and although the British had a tendency to treat them with good-natured contempt, they behaved themselves better than we did, and they were just not interested in suicide. Their leader and exemplar was Prince Valerio Borghese, a pale, dark, military-looking man who could have served as a model for any young Prussian officer. Although he had always held himself coolly aloof both from Mussolini and the Germans he was not prepared to let himself be used by the British. The group of officers with him were completely under his control; like him, they were calm, dignified, and apparently indifferent to the camp life. Every time I saw Prince Borghese on my morning exercise I felt that there went the very best type of Roman gentleman and the finest anti-Prussian Prussian I had ever come across.

An Italian the British certainly never took seriously was the white-haired Marshal Graziani, notorious for his tremendous strategic plans, all of which were utterly impossible because— if for no other reason—there weren't enough Divisions in the world to carry them out. He was a General who—in his own opinion at least—would never have lost a battle if only he had had enough troops to fight it with. His great activity in the camp consisted of exploiting his connections with the Vatican, which he did through his wife. If he had any sort of reputation at all with the British, this activity certainly did not enhance it. However, he seems to have met with at least a modicum of success, for one day a large cake arrived for him from the Vatican.

Another Italian in Cine Città was Leto, the mysterious chief of the *Ovra*, or Italian Secret Police. In appearance he looked a fat bureaucrat, but actually he was the descendant of an ancient Sicilian patrician house. When you were his guest— as I often had been—you made no mention of politics, though

17

it was notorious that it was due largely to Leto and Bocchini between them that Italian Fascism had managed to last as long as it did. Leto was a genius as a policeman. At first he had been held in an Italian prison, but in view of the composition of the new Italian Government that would sooner or later have meant his death. At my first interrogation I mentioned him to my examiner—not out of any great feeling of friendship for policemen, but because of the pleasant times I had spent as a guest under his roof. At first my examiner didn't know who Leto was (not for nothing was Leto chief of the *Ovra*!), but as soon as he realized the man's importance he had him transferred to Cine Città and a few days later I spotted him at morning exercise. He looked tired and overworked, though at that time he had nothing to do at all. I saw him for a few days in this way and then I never saw him again.

One evening when I was watching the sun sink behind the Neapolitan hills as usual—a scene so familiar by this time that I could have painted it from memory, but one that never lost its attraction—I heard voices near my cell, and two of them were those of women. This feminine invasion of a camp which up to then had been completely male struck me as a good omen, but then I heard one of the women refer to "the *Reichsführer*", and immediately I realized who she was.

Frau Himmler and her daughter Gudrun had come to stay with us as guests of the British. Some obscure S.S. leader had betrayed their hide-out in South Tirol, and the British had been compelled to arrest her. Actually, as a prisoner she was something of an embarrassment to them, and they didn't know quite what to do with her. Although they believed her to be another Ilse Koch, their long and deeply rooted traditions of chivalry forbade them to treat her as, for example, the Germans had treated Princess Mafalda of Italy, who had died in Buchenwald concentration camp in the charitable arms of a Berlin whore.

I was one of those the British questioned about Frau Himmler, and I discovered that they had some idea that she was a female devil in human form, and that every night after dinner she had presented her husband with fresh lists of people to be arrested, and with new tortures to be tried out on the female prisoners. I did my best to correct that absurd impression. I pointed out that although you could think what you liked of the woman's character, I happened to know that she had not been allowed even to mention politics. As far as Himmler was concerned, she belonged in the kitchen, and perhaps in bed as well, but that it was quite inconceivable that he had ever said a word to her about the internal arrangements of his concentration camps.

It was only in Cine Città that Frau Himmler heard of the death of her husband, and her immediate comment was: "I thank God that my husband is now beyond the reach of all the attacks and slanders to which he would have been subjected."

She and her daughter were the only women in the camp, and no special arrangements had been made for them. Every time one of them went to the lavatory a soldier had to accompany her. And then the food! It was bad enough for a man, and if I had had courage enough I would have done what little Gudrun Himmler did—go on hunger strike. As a result of her strike she did obtain better food for herself and her mother, and after a week or two they were transferred elsewhere.

Soon after my arrival in the camp I learned something at first hand of the methods of the British Intelligence Service, and the evening sunset watching and the monotonous morning walk were no longer the only incidents in my dull days. The name of my examiner was Bridge, Major Bridge. I learned that at once, for the first thing he did was to introduce himself politely. Rather unnecessarily, and with the usual slight bow, I informed him that my name was Dollmann, Colonel Dollmann. I had a good look at him. For the time being at least he was to represent the British Empire as far as I was concerned. I must say that my first impression was quite favourable.

He was a new type of policeman for me, and I had met a few by then. For example, one of them was Heydrich, the *Gestapo* chief. Now there was a man clearly meant to be murdered by someone or other. He was a daemonic personality, a Lucifer with cold blue eyes. And his methods were in keeping. The *Gestapo* was not subtle or refined; it was brutal with a shocking and at the same time horribly fascinating cruelty. It relied on brute force and not on intelligence, and Heydrich was its worthy representative. That he died as he did was right and proper. For him to have died in his bed like any ordinary man—though, of course, a lot of ordinary men had been dying elsewhere—would have been out of keeping.

Bocchini was another policeman, but a very different type indeed. He always reminded me of a historical left-over from the days of Ancient Rome, and he did for Mussolini what he would have done for, say, the Emperor Augustus—spared him the nuisance of continued attempts at assassination. The ancient Roman chiefs of police had used islands in the Black Sea as banishment spots. Bocchini used the Lipari islands in the Mediterranean; his organization, the *Ovra*, under Leto, was not brutal like the *Gestapo* and its methods were very different.

It did not go in for vast round-ups or mass beating orgies. Instead it tapped telephone lines on a large scale; it kept a close eye on the mistresses of its clients; and it bribed prostitutes, pimps, brothel keepers and aristocrats. Its work began with the first kiss and was by no means concluded in bed. No other secret police used quite such methods, but there, no other secret police had quite the same successes. Bocchini knew human nature very intimately, but few people recognized in the pleasure-loving Grand Seigneur the last of the great European police chiefs.

Allan Dulles was another policeman I got to know. He always struck me as a leather-faced Puritan archangel who had fled from the European sink of iniquity on the *Mayflower* and now returned to scourge the sinners of the old world. He was incorruptible and totally humourless. During the capitulation negotiations he had to come up against Wolff, who believed in God. He was faced with a riddle which seemed insoluble. After that his Secret Service began to use different methods.

Bridge was a ginger-haired fellow with a pale complexion and a crop of freckles. He wore gold-rimmed spectacles and looked like a University professor, though rather a young one. He spoke quietly and agreeably in fluent Italian, without a trace of accent as far as I could tell, and his manner seemed to me a trifle old world.

"Sit down, Herr Dollmann. Now tell me: how on earth did you get into this hole?"

But he didn't wait for any explanation I might have had to offer and he went on at once:

"I find it very odd," and he pretended not to be studying my face, but I could see that he was.

"What do you find so odd?" I inquired.

"Oh, perhaps it's nothing really. It's just that an intelligent man like you should find himself in your present position."

"I can easily explain that," I replied. The "intelligent man" bit was obviously not flattery and on that account I felt very flattered. I told him about my work in the Vatican, and how my linguistic abilities had first brought me into contact with Roman high society—and then with politicians.

"It was at that time that I first met Hitler. He came to see Mussolini, and my services were called in as interpreter."

Bridge was still fiddling with his fountain-pen, but I could see that he was listening carefully. Once again he raised his finger.

"We know all about that, Herr Dollmann," he said amiably. I must have showed surprise, for he went on explanatorily: "I was often close to you Herr Dollmann and I made a point of studying you. For one thing I noticed that you were very fond of pineapple."

He laughed, no doubt at the look of astonishment on my face, and put down the fountain-pen. "We actually know you quite well and it's just as well that you're telling the truth. And now we'd rather like you to tell us something about the execution of the hostages in the Ardeatine caves."

I was about to protest, but again that upraised finger stopped me.

"Of course, we know that you had nothing directly to do with that affair, but you must understand that there are certain inquiries we have to make."

"Yes," I said. "I understand that of course, but I really had nothing whatever to do with it either directly or indirectly."

He had been very considerate in his manner up to then but as soon as he mentioned that matter it reminded me that I was really in front of an officer of the Intelligence Service and not a pleasant University professor, and that the Intelligence Service, like all similar institutions, had ways and means of persuading

21

unwilling prisoners to talk. I also remembered the American military police with their chin-straps framing their brutal faces, and the mocking way they had laughed as the Italian mob bombarded us with stones and rotten eggs whilst Wolff was saying good-bye to his wife and children.

Bridge got up as an indication that our first interview was at an end.

"I'm sorry that I shall have to trouble you again," he said with a smile, "but we were at war, you know."

"Of course," I replied, and I got up too and was about to turn to the door when he put out his hand. We shook hands and I went back to my cell.

During the next few days life in the camp was rather peaceful. From time to time Englishmen would come to my cell to chat to me. The stale perfume left behind by Beatrice Cenci didn't seem to disturb them. Sometimes they would bring along a bottle of whisky or a bottle of Frascati and we would talk about Italian literature, humanism in general, the Third Reich, the psychological basis of Fascism—about a great number of things in fact but never about any concerning my present situation. Unlike the Americans the English had books of their own, and a good many of them already occupied a place in the literature of the world. They were good enough to lend me some of them.

On one occasion Bridge called me to his office.

"You probably find life rather boring here, Herr Dollmann," he said. "I've a little job you may find interesting."

He indicated a file of papers on the desk in front of him.

"I'd like you to look through this material and tell me what you think of it."

"Why, of course," I replied. For one thing I quite liked Bridge and I was therefore willing to do him a favour, and secondly life was a bit boring and anything of interest was welcome.

"It isn't an order, you understand. You would just be obliging me."

"What is it then?"

Bridge looked out of the window.

"It's the diary of Count Ciano," he said.

I took the file and went back to my cell. Every evening one or other of the British officers would come to my cell for a

chat, but Ciano's diary was never mentioned. One evening
Bridge himself arrived with a bottle of whisky, but he also
made no reference to the matter in hand and it was only about
ten days later when I returned the material to him in his
office that it was mentioned again. He was standing at the
window.

"Ah, yes! Well, what do you think of it?"

I sat down and took the cigarette he offered me.

"I think you've done it very well indeed," I said.

Bridge grinned and seemed a little embarrassed.

"What do you mean exactly?" he asked.

For a moment I was afraid that I had been too frank. After
all, if I became awkward they could always send me back to
the Americans, and that prospect was not inviting. But Bridge
was smiling quite amiably from where he stood by the window
so I decided not to withdraw.

"For an innocent it would all sound very convincing no
doubt, but for anyone who happened to know Ciano at all well
it would be absurd."

He laughed.

"All right, Herr Dollmann. But tell me: what about the
general style? Doesn't that strike you as authentic?"

"Yes," I said. "It does."

And it really did. Whoever had "edited" this diary of Ciano
must have had some of Ciano's material at his disposal, but it
was quite certain that half the stuff I had just read hadn't come
from Ciano at all. In secret I was rather impressed: I wouldn't
have credited the British with so much guile. But perhaps in
the circumstances it was a little risky for me to talk so openly.
Major Bridge seemed to have the same feeling, for he came
towards the desk and changed the subject abruptly:

"Thank you for letting me know your opinion. By the way,
you can set your mind at rest about the shooting of those
hostages. Kappler himself has declared that you had nothing
whatever to do with it."

"I said that in the beginning," I replied. That remark was
a bit impertinent too, but Bridge didn't react to it.

"We knew it already," he said, "but we have our instructions
to carry out just the same as you had."

There was a flush of embarrassment on his face, but at least the answer was fair enough. I said no more but just sat there and waited whilst he walked up and down between the desk and the window. Finally he stopped at the desk.

"All right," he said. "All that remains is for you to be cleared by the Allied Commission, and then . . ."

"And then?" I repeated.

He ignored me and pressed a bell. A sergeant appeared and took me back to my cell. It was the first time that Bridge had been at all brusque with me, but I knew whose fault that was.

Incidentally, that was not the end of my literary labours on behalf of the Intelligence Service. It was summer now, a real merciless Roman summer. Longingly I looked through the wire grid over the window of my star dressing-room towards the distant horizon beyond which lay the Sea of Ostia and its strand. No doubt there were the usual shouts of "What, darling! You here!" They were just too far away for me to hear, and this time they wouldn't be for Ciano and his friends, but for the Johnnies, Jims and Jacks of the American forces of occupation. After all, what had they won the war for? And a little to the left I could just make out the sulphur spa of Acque Albule. No doubt the cream of Roman society was still enjoying itself there too, but in a strictly private world of its own, fenced off from the rest of humanity—*per il corpo diplomatico!* Black-tongued chows, slim salukis and fat little pekes would still be guarding their diplomatic mistresses, but now without interference from Argos and Cuno, my two German sheep-dogs, miscalled Alsatians by the rest of the world. Owing to their tendency to mistake lap dogs for balls of wool made animated for their benefit, they had caused more than one near-diplomatic incident. But that was all over now.

It grew hotter and hotter and the days rolled by dateless and anonymous. Only once did heavy rain clouds roll up from the north and on that day two British orderlies came into my cell carrying a brand-new typewriter and a pile of paper which they put down on the table and went away without offering any explanation. The explanation followed a little later. An officer of the Intelligence Service came in. It was not Major Bridge.

"It's going to rain, Herr Dollmann," he observed.

24

I nodded.

"It certainly looks like it," I agreed.

"Just as it did a year ago," he went on. "Right to the day. Don't you remember?"

I shook my head. No, I didn't remember particularly.

"But to-day's July 20th, Herr Dollmann. Surely you haven't forgotten?"

I had. It didn't matter much to me here what day of the week it was, or what date. But now I remembered. Just a year ago I had accompanied Mussolini on his return from a visit of inspection to his newly-formed Italian Divisions in Germany. He was on his way to the Rastenburg Headquarters of the Führer, where Adolf's last miracle had just occurred, though we didn't know anything about that then.

"I expect you're bored with nothing to do, Herr Dollmann, and we should be very much interested in your story. It would be highly confidential of course, and we should be very grateful to you. And naturally you could keep a copy for yourself."

I gradually began to see what he was after. And so it turned out: he wanted the story of the Duce's visit to Rastenburg just after the attempt on Hitler's life on July 20th. Well, why not? It had been a historical day and my memory of it was still green, but I wasn't getting any younger and my memory wasn't getting any better, so it might be as well if I put it down on paper. Obediently therefore I sat down at the typewriter and July 20th 1945 went by rapidly. I made a copy for myself and the British kept their word once again. I still have that copy. Here's the contents of it:—

The special train which was carrying Mussolini and his suite, including myself, to Rastenburg to visit Hitler at his headquarters there, suddenly pulled up in open country. All the blinds were down and no one knew why we had stopped. There was a good deal of excited whispering but no reliable information. It was pitch dark, but no air raids had been notified and as far as we knew—and hoped—the Russians were still a long way away. However, we were strictly warned not to raise the blinds or hang around in the corridors. After a while the train went on again. It was not until two o'clock in the afternoon

when the train ran into Rastenburg Station that we learned
what had happened. Hitler was there in person to greet us.

"Duce! Only a little while ago I experienced the greatest
piece of good fortune in my life."

Hitler was very pale, but he seemed quite calm. The Italian
thus greeted still had no idea what it was all about, and even
the fact that Hitler put out his left hand instead of his right
did not strike any of us as significant at the moment. Behind
Hitler a particularly imposing retinue nodded heads in devout
and enthusiastic agreement. There was the Reich's Marshal
himself. Lohengrin—I mean Goering—in a white uniform
which made him look fatter than ever. Ribbentrop, nervous
and jumpy in a field-grey uniform. Martin Bormann looking
like a sinister bull terrier in his uniform. And Himmler was
there too, with his cold eyes glittering through his pince-nez.

Perhaps the decisive victory over the Red Army had been
won? Or perhaps the Allies had granted Hitler the fulfilment
of his old wish-dream and made him Supreme Commander of
all the forces of the West for the crusade against Bolshevism?
Or had the secret weapons we had heard so much about proved
their existence and their quality at last?

The short journey to the Führer's Headquarters brought us
the real explanation: Count Stauffenberg's attempt on Hitler's
life had failed, and everyone regarded it as a miracle.

A fine grey rain fell steadily over the gloomy pines and on
to excited adjutants who brought the still unusually quiet
Führer the latest reports. It was running in little trickles down
Himmler's pasty face as he took his leave to speed off to Berlin
to dip his soft white hands into the blood bath being prepared
there. The retinue broke up. The two Foreign Ministers, the
German Ribbentrop and the Italian, Count Mazzolini, went
off to discuss their affairs, and Hitler led his fellow dictator into
the building in which the explosion had taken place.

"I was standing at this table," Hitler declared dramatically,
"and here at my feet the bomb exploded."

For a moment or two there was silence as the two dictators
looked around at the chaos and debris.

Then Hitler repeated what he had previously said about the
great stroke of good fortune that had once again saved his life

and expressed his conviction that that same good fortune would now stand them both in good stead until final victory.

The Duce agreed enthusiastically. What else could he do? And in any case, he needed something to cheer him up. Perhaps in that short silent pause his own memory had gone back for just a year when the goddess of fortune had deserted him for good and all in Rome—unless you can count the short visit she paid him in his exile on Lake Garda. But at least she had just stood by his friend here in Rastenburg, and that was a bit of luck for him too.

The two Foreign Ministers without a foreign policy returned from their pointless discussion, during which the far-better informed Italian had warned his German colleague of the approaching collapse of the satellite front in the Balkans and in particular of the coming defection of Roumania. The optimistic Ribbentrop refused to be depressed, or at least to appear depressed.

"I feel like a champion boxer going forward for the last round," he said. "Of course I have taken heavy punishment, but believe me I shall enter the final struggle with iron nerves and complete confidence. A miracle has just saved the life of our Führer here, and a miracle will yet save us in the Balkans. Readiness is everything that counts now."

Perhaps he really was optimistic. In any case, he pretended to be. The Italians were not, and they didn't bother to pretend to be.

The second act of the performance began at the heavily-laden table in the Führer bunker when "five o'clock tea" was served —as usual by S.S. men in white waiters' jackets. A growing company sat down on either side of the two dictators. The conversation was loud and confident. Goering was as boastful as ever. Bormann talked about the Party. Ribbentrop held forth on foreign policy.

"My Führer," declared Goering. "Now you know why your brave troops had to give way again and again in the East! They were betrayed by the Generals. But now our undefeated Divisions, and above all my own 'Hermann Goering Division', will drive forward into the heart of the enemy and the whole front will advance again."

Admiral Dönitz, who was also there, was not to be outdone by Hermann: "Through me, my Führer, your devoted blue-jackets announce their firm determination to fight on to victory. 'Nearer to the enemy!' is their motto. Now the Generals are no longer there to betray us the seas will be ours."

And Martin Bormann: "This criminal attempt has united the whole German people behind you, my Führer, like a strong fortress. Now that the Generals and their aristocratic fellow conspirators are no longer able to sabotage my work, all Party Comrades will fight on with renewed strength for you and your mission."

Ribbentrop: "My Führer, my friend Count Mazzolini has just informed me that the political situation in the Balkans requires our close attention. But after this great day everything will change for the better now that the treacherous machinations of the Generals and the reactionary clique in the Wilhelm Strasse have been brought to an end. My diplomats in the Balkans will see to it that we hold our positions with an iron hand."

All of them were suddenly relieved of their worries and anxieties concerning the past, the present and the future. All the mistakes, bloomers and defeats could now be put down to the treacherous Generals. Although the speakers hated each other, loathed each other and intrigued against each other whenever they got the chance, to-day they were all in agreement. In the general hubbub Mussolini's War Minister, the grey-haired Marshal Graziani vainly tried to get in the story of his own escape in Addis Ababa.

Only the two Italian diplomats did not join in. Count Mazzolini and his ambassador Anfuso were too much occupied with their own discussion, and that will hardly have been so carefree. Those who knew the handsome Filippo Anfuso might well have guessed his thoughts now: at last a German July 25th! and punishment for all the arrogance and rudeness the Germans had shown to their Italian allies, and for all the humiliations they had made them suffer! Perhaps henceforth the Germans would not be quite so cock-a-hoop after their own experience —even if Hitler had, by a miracle, escaped.

The only one present who seemed unmoved by it all was Vittorio Mussolini, the Duce's shallow son. There he sat smiling all over his face and eating the Führer's cake whilst the white-jacketed S.S. men, astonished at such a vast appetite, served him with one piece after the other.

The Duce himself was ill at ease. With his Latin flair for atmospheric disturbance he was growing more and more nervous, wriggling around on his chair, pecking without interest at the food on his plate and fortifying himself—very much against his usual habits—with brandy. Several times he suggested to his host and fellow dictator that the party should now break up, but in vain. No power on earth could stop Hitler going through with his performance.

The obsequious flattery of his subordinates had made no particular impression on him. He had ignored Graziani's attempts to get a word in and he had paid no attention to the whispered conversation of the Italian Foreign Minister with his Berlin Ambassador. Only with a nod of the head had he instructed the S.S. waiters to keep Vittorio Mussolini's plate filled.

There he sat and brooded, his right arm hanging down inertly, his expressionless eyes directed into some mysterious distance, his left hand fiddling with the coloured tablets, green, blue and yellow, provided by his personal physician Dr. Morell to pep him up. Gradually his mood affected the company, and around him the talk and the boasting ceased. Finally there was silence altogether and then followed tense, unquiet minutes before the expected storm broke. The rain fell ceaselessly outside, running down the window panes, and inside all eyes were fixed anxiously on the brooding figure of the Führer. Only he could relieve the gathering tension which he himself had created. At last it came.

"Never have I felt more strongly that Providence is at my side," he began in a monotonous voice. "The miracle which has just taken place has convinced me more than ever that I am called to higher things and that I will lead the German people to the greatest victory in all their history."

Then he turned to Mussolini:

"Duce! Believe me: we shall be victorious!"

Mussolini stopped playing nervously with crumbs on the tablecloth and nodded enthusiastically. And then Hitler went on in a louder and more excited voice so that even Vittorio stopped eating cake at last and Graziani's waving hair almost stood on end.

"But I will first destroy all those criminal elements who dare to place themselves in the path of Providence. I shall crush them absolutely. Traitors to their own people deserve a shameful death—and they shall have it! I will take vengeance for this hour on all those who are found to be guilty, and on their families too, as far as they assisted them. I will wipe out this brood of vipers which seeks to prevent Germany's victory. I will sweep them off the face of the earth. You can all rely on that."

He had begun in an almost toneless voice, but gradually it had risen until finally it became a screech. In speaking he had half risen from his seat and his shifty eyes flickered in a dead-white face as he shrieked his way to the end of his monologue. Where had such tones been heard before? Suddenly it seemed that it was no longer Adolf Hitler, the Führer of the Third Reich, the greatest persecutor of Jews since the days of Nebuchadnezzar, and his features began to take on the threatening appearance of another great leader of peoples, the leader of that very people whose destruction Hitler had sworn to bring about. The accents were those of Moses on his return from Mount Sinai after his colloquy with Jehova, the God of vengeance:

"And if men strive together . . . and any mischief follow, then thou shalt give life for life, eye for eye, tooth for tooth, hand for hand, foot for foot, burning for burning, wound for wound, stripe for stripe."

But then with beat of wings the Erinyes of the Third Reich left the close and humid atmosphere of the tea-room and the vision was gone, leaving behind a motionless figure, bent forward over the table. With white face and empty eyes Hitler stared in front of him at nothing.

It was Mussolini who broke the spell. Looking his friend in the face and taking his hand he smiled and almost as though with an effort Hitler returned to the world around him. The two dictators rose to their feet and the door opened letting in a cooling breeze from the east. Hitler still did not know what was happening in Berlin, but now his only care was for the well-being of his friend and he called at once for Mussolini's warm cloak.

"The Duce must not catch cold."

His role was now only that of the thoughtful host, and it was such sudden displays of consideration and charm that confused the historical picture of his character. The overworked word "daemonism" is not enough to explain the man's nature completely.

In the meantime the conversation had been haltingly resumed. Keitel and Graziani had withdrawn for military discussions. At last the long-expected call from Berlin came through. Hitler hurried to the telephone. Goebbels was at the other end of the line. Mussolini and I were invited to listen in to this all-important conversation. Goebbels reported the great change that had come over the situation there and handed the line over to Major Remer, the Commander of the Berlin Watch Battalion, on whose attitude everything now depended.

Major Remer informed Hitler of the order which had been given him to occupy the Reich's Chancellory after the report of the Führer's death.

"Major Remer," said Hitler, "can you hear my voice?"

"Yes, my Führer."

"Major Remer, the Commander-in-Chief of the German Armed Forces is now speaking to you and I give you the following instructions . . ."

"Yes, my Führer," interrupted Remer.

And then Hitler gave his orders: firstly, secondly, thirdly . . .

We know what happened after that: the Watch Battalion marched to the War Office in the Bendler Strasse to arrest the conspirators of July 20th.

Hitler turned to Mussolini with a beaming face. Providence must also have been beaming. In Berlin Goebbels beamed. No doubt Major Remer was beaming too—he had just been promoted. Before long the goddesses of vengeance were to have every opportunity of beaming too. The flabby hands of Heinrich Himmler were soon to turn against the unfortunate old Field Marshal von Witzleben and his friends. Mercy was out of the question and a terrible end awaited them all.

Now the Führer had more important things to occupy his mind than a visitor from the unimportant provincial town of Salo on Lake Garda, and the usual farewell ceremony was hurried through. Off went the visitors to the station with their host. The sky was overclouded again and the tea party drove through the wet pine woods to where Mussolini's special train was waiting.

At the station an old man with his peaked cap pulled even further down over his eyes than usual stretched out a shaking left hand to another old man. The sun had disappeared completely now and the rain began to fall more and more heavily on the two dictators. The usual oaths of mutual loyalty were left out this time. The thing had to be cut short, it was raining really hard. And what use would they have been in any case? Perhaps they both realized in their hearts that they would never see each other again.

That was my description of the meeting of the two dictators on July 20th 1944, and that evening I handed it to the grateful agents of the Intelligence Service for their "highly confidential" use. But unlike the Axis partners, it appeared that there were no secrets between the Allies. Hitler had never told his Italian partners what he intended to do, or only when it was too late, and Mussolini didn't warn his German partners of his approaching drive into Greece. With the British and the Americans it was different, and in July 1947 when I read *Germany's Underground* by Allan W. Dulles I found he had made full use of my July 20th story—without acknowledgement and without payment of a fee.

By this time I was allowed to meet Wolff again and we walked around a good deal together. The new Italian Premier was Parri. Wolff and I knew him; in fact we knew him very well. After the release of Mussolini he had become second-in-command of the Italian Resistance. In civilian life he had been the representative of an American wireless firm in Milan. He was a man of limited intelligence. A few months before the collapse of Italy and our capitulation he had been arrested by the Security Service.

On March 3rd when I was in Lugano negotiating with the representative of Dulles concerning the signing of the German capitulation in Italy, a piece of paper was pushed across the table to me. On it was the name Parri and I was informed that the Americans would regard it as a proof of our good will if we handed him over to them, and this we did. Dulles, I know, regarded him as the future strong man of Italy, and Parri subsequently became the first Premier of Italy after the Liberation. In reality the man was a complete frost.

Wolff and I wrote to Parri from the camp reminding him of the circumstances of his release and suggesting a *quid pro quo*, but by that time Parri apparently preferred to have nothing more to do with Germans, and we received no reply.

One day, after we had all been before the Allied Commission of Inquiry and I had been acquitted of all charges in connection with executions, atrocities and so on, Wolff greeted me with great enthusiasm when I met him for our usual morning walk.

"I'm getting out of here," he shouted joyfully even before he had come up to me. "Just imagine, Eugenio!" he exclaimed. "My plane leaves for the North to-day."

We had been acquitted by the Allied Commission it was true, but for all that the general atmosphere did not encourage me in the belief that all was now forgiven and forgotten.

"Whereabouts in the north, *Herr General?*" I inquired cautiously.

My tone was not lost on him.

"Ach Dollmann! You're much too pessimistic. It's going to be all right. Would you like me to take any letters for you. The others have given me theirs."

I was still sceptical but I thought he might as well take a letter from me to my relatives.

Later on I saw Major Bridge standing in the doorway of his office. He called me over to him.

"Have you seen Wolff to-day?" he asked.

"Yes," I replied. "He's on top of the world. He's getting out of here and going home."

"He's not, you know," said Bridge bluntly, and then he added in an undertone: "Actually I shouldn't say this to you,

33

Dollmann, but between you and me he'll wish himself back in Cine Città before he's much older."

"Where's he going then?" I asked with an under-current of anxiety. After all, if it happened to Wolff it could happen to me.

"Nuremberg."

I was about to say something, but the finger rose. "Incidentally, you needn't worry. You're not in the party. And don't say anything to him about it, if you please."

It was politely put, but it was an order; the tone was enough to tell me that. Later on I met Wolff again.

"Are you coming along?" he asked cheerfully.

"No," I said. Major Bridge was still standing in the door of his office. "And if I were you I shouldn't set my hopes too high."

A jeep with a couple of men in it drove up for Wolff. He laughed happily and shook hands with me:

"Good-bye, Eugenio. I'll be seeing you again in Germany."

"Yes, of course. Good-bye, *Herr General*."

Wolff ended that day in a cell in Nuremberg Prison where the war criminals were being brought together for trial.

It was already October and Cine Città was gradually beginning to empty. Not only the prisoners but also the officers of the Intelligence Service were shaking the dust of the place from their boots. Incidentally, it was mud now.

One day a jeep drove up to my cell and Major Bridge got out and came in to see me.

"We're moving on," he said. "I'm sorry in a way. It hasn't been bad here."

I didn't altogether agree with him, and when he expressed the hope that I had not been too bored I was unable to reassure him.

"We're closing down this camp. After all, you can't stay in a film-star's dressing-room for ever," he said, and he laughed.

I smiled a trifle sourly. "What will happen to me then?"

"Well, I've written a letter to Ascona about you. I don't think you'll find it too bad there."

"Ascona has a reputation of being a starvation camp," I said.

"Yes," agreed the major, "I know. "But my authority over you has ended."

He went outside and came back with a military raincoat over his arm. It had no badges.

"I thought you'd like this," he said. "You haven't a raincoat and I believe there's going to be a good deal of rain."

He handed me the raincoat.

"You couldn't possibly have given me anything more useful," I said gratefully.

He grinned to hide his embarrassment and held out 1 ' hand.

"It's a good coat," he said. "I hope we'll meet again under more agreeable circumstances, Herr Dollmann."

"I hope so too, Major Bridge. And many thanks."

We shook hands. When I got into the jeep with my things and it drove off he stood in front of my cell and saluted.

It was already raining and my new raincoat began to darken. The jeep drove through the camp gates and turned in the direction of Ascona.

Chapter II

THE POOR IMITATION

ASCONA seemed to be intended as an Allied imitation of Dachau, but although the victors undoubtedly tried hard they didn't altogether succeed. Personally I'm very glad they didn't. I had no desire to spend an indefinite period of my life in a really authentic copy of the place.

My initial satisfaction soon gave way to a permanent feeling of empty rolling in my stomach, though I told myself that even that was better than the gas cellars in the original article. A consolation, but not enough to make up for the fact that the amount of food they provided us with in this very mixed camp was barely enough to keep body and soul together.

We didn't have the far-famed Italian sunshine to help us over the difficulty. Instead of that there were dark clouds overhead which emptied rain on us and turned the ground into a morass of muddy clay. Our tents—at least in Dachau they had had wooden huts—were pitched on a hill. During storms we would lie wrapped up in our blankets and find it difficult to believe that our last hour was not at hand. And when it just rained—and it just rained quite a lot in those autumn months, our tents, complete with everything in them, slowly slid down the hillside towards the sea. The next morning our first job was to carry them back up the hill again and erect them as best we could in the mud so that the wind should have a better chance of repeating the process up there the following night.

It was pretty grim, but no one maltreated us; we hadn't to stay in the open for hours and do knee-bends; no one was carted off to the gas chambers; no one was beaten up; and no one was hanged. But our food was rationed down to the lowest possible limit, and very carefully at that.

We had to wash ourselves in the open air, a process of hardening perhaps, particularly when it was cold—and it was cold.

36

We would line up, stripped to the waist, in front of the gutter-like troughs in the wash place and let ice-cold water run over us out of a rusty pipe.

The latrines were in the open air too of course and they were in charge of a former good-conduct prisoner from—yes, Dachau. He was also in charge of the whole camp. There we would crouch like starving sparrows on a wire and hand over our valuables to this gentleman, and in return we would receive a little more of the watery, half-frozen peasoup we had to exist on. After that, much strengthened, we would be back in the latrines again to discover that the wheel had now turned full circle: valuables, peasoup, latrines, valuables.

Our head supervisor was a man of parts. He had distinguished himself in Dachau as a prisoner and good-conduct man, and as a reward the Nazis had sent him to the front in a punishment company. This company then fell into Allied hands so that this gentleman once again found himself in a camp; not as a prisoner this time, but as a warder. He was not inhuman and thanks to his powers under the Allied authority he would, as I have said, exchange our valuables for more peasoup. I got on quite well with him until all my valuables had gone. I was not the only one to whom that happened and when the reserves of valuables in Ascona were exhausted I was privileged to observe members of Italian high society going around half-naked. Trousers they still had, and usually an overcoat, but that was about all. The other things they had always regarded as essential to refined living were missing. It was after this that the peasoup war started in real earnest.

Every evening we received a portion of this horrible mess. Some of the officers there had made primitive scales out of old bully-beef tins—their contents had never had any relation to our feeding—and pieces of wood, and with these scales each man's portion was weighed. If it turned out that someone had even an ounce more than his normal share the discussions would begin: ought he to divide the extra portion into two, three, four, or perhaps more parts in order that each of those who had received less should get their fair share? In the end the surplus—if that's the right word—was usually put in the kitty and a game of bridge organized. The winner took the kitty.

The men didn't bother about such refinements. They poured all their peas out into one container and then each man helped himself.

But there were those, both officers and men, who were not interested in this pease-pudding as food. They were the helpless addicts of nicotine. As soon as they got their share they would run around until they had succeeded in exchanging it for cigarettes, though how they did it is a mystery to me. And a still greater mystery is how they managed to survive at all. They were rarely if ever seen in the latrines—since they didn't eat—and they nourished themselves by smoking. How a man can survive on poison I don't know. I am a smoker myself, but I have never doubted the assertion of the scientists that nicotine is a poison.

In the meantime winter had arrived. It was colder than ever. The latrines and the washing place were ice-rinks, and the pease-pudding was more watery and icy than ever. It was at this point that I decided to remove myself from Ascona, and the one and only heroic period of my life opened up. Major Bridge and his raincoat were responsible for it.

However, I was not responsible for leaving Ascona. The Allied authorities closed down the camp and transferred us all to a much larger camp at Rimini, which held hundreds of S.S., Intelligence, Security-Service and Party leaders in addition to ordinary prisoners of war, both officers and men. When we were taken into the camp, who should I see standing with arms akimbo at the gate but the former chief of our Security Service in Milan, a fellow named Rauf. His position in Milan had been the same as Kappler's in Rome. Here he was camp supervisor. He spotted me at once.

"Dollmann!" he exclaimed. "Well, would you believe it! If there's any man I could have done without . . ."

I felt exactly the same way about him, but in view of his position in the camp I thought it better to keep the fact to myself. If I needed anything further at all to turn me against this mass camp in Rimini it was to find one of my most disagreeable acquaintances in charge, and no doubt anxious to show the British how a Nazi could establish order and discipline even in a chaotic dump like Rimini.

My determination to escape became firmer and firmer, but as yet I wasn't sure how it was to be done. I also had a feeling —though it may have been baseless—that I was being threatened by someone or other, and as I did nothing practical about it, it soon developed into a fixed idea. My general discomfort was added to by the fact that the feeding here—though it takes some believing—was even worse than in Ascona. It wasn't possible to squabble solemnly here about surplus pease-pudding —there just wasn't any.

I tried to find others to join in the escape plan I hadn't worked out yet, but I hadn't much talent for conspiracy. In consequence a new terror was added to my existence: I was afraid that my conspiratorial efforts would be discovered and that I should be condemned to cleaning out the latrines. This made me more than ever anxious to get out. First of all I didn't know how to get near to the wire without immediately awakening suspicion so I decided to approach a number of important prisoners whose tent was nearer the wire than mine. Kappler was one of them and I felt certain that he would gladly join in any escape venture. In my opinion he was quite certainly due for the high jump when they got round to him and therefore he ought to welcome even the slenderest chance of escape.

But I was wrong. Kappler explained to me that in his opinion the honour of a German officer and gentleman required that he should obey orders and submit to his fate. I, on the other hand, felt that I was entitled to choose my own end to the best of my ability and I wasn't keen on dying of hunger in Rimini camp, so I gave Kappler up as a bad job and tried the others. But with no better success. They weren't interested, or may be they had no confidence in me.

After that I sank to the level of N.C.O.s. At first they stared at me as though I had taken leave of my senses, but when I explained to them that I spoke fluent Italian they became enthusiastic. After that the preparations for escape began in earnest. On the day we had decided to make our break I made an effigy with straw in my—I can't really call it a bed; it was only a couple of planks—kipping place, covered it up with blankets and put my uniform cap on top of it. I had to sacrifice my greatcoat and that pained me. It had been made by the finest—and most expensive—tailor in Rome and it had cost a mint of money. In a flash I realized how much pease-pudding I could get for it and just for a moment I almost gave up my plans. I also sacrificed my last silk shirt, and I poured a bottle of eau de Cologne over it to counteract the smell of straw. Upon my word, the final result wasn't bad at all. My satisfaction was diminished only by the thought of what would happen to me if the guards found out too soon.

The security measures at Rimini camp were not slipshod. They had got us there and they intended to keep us there, and the camp was very closely watched and guarded. It was surrounded by high barbed-wire fences and every three hundred yards or so there was a watch-tower complete with heavy machine-gun post whilst searchlights swept the ground around the camp at regular intervals after dark. And there was nothing to be done with the guards. They were Poles and far from kindly disposed towards us.

One of our party had calculated that our searchlight swept a particular piece of ground every three minutes. In this space of three minutes we had to be through the wire and far enough away for the searchlight not to pick us out when it swept round again. That day went slowly, but at last evening came and it grew dark. The searchlights were switched on and outside my tent I heard whispers. My companions were ready. We got down to it in a line before the wire and waited our chance. The fellow next to me had a strange instrument of steel with him.

"What's that?" I asked.

"Wire-cutters," he answered. "How do you think we're going to get through the stuff without?"

There was something in that.

"Where did you get them?" I whispered.

"Found them," he grunted. Which was a good enough answer to a silly and unnecessary question. The thought struck me, and so I decided to stop talking and accept the fact.

The nearest searchlight moved along ahead of us over the ground, lighting everything up in an eerie, milky glare, and then went off towards the sea.

"Now," hissed the N.C.O., and I gave a sign to the waiting men and we dashed forward to the wire. They were good wire-cutters wherever he had got them and they did the job rapidly, which was just as well, for there was no time to lose now. Out of a feeling of higher morality I waited until all the others were through, but all the time—and it seemed a long time—I was haunted by thoughts that the searchlight would return before its time and that the Poles would set the dogs on us, as they did whenever the occasion arose—and then I crawled through myself. Everyone else got through all right but when my turn came I had to slide into a puddle of muddy clay, which did Major Bridge's raincoat no good. I picked myself up and was about to walk off thankfully when the N.C.O. who had appointed himself commander of our undertaking snarled: "Down you bloody fool!"

I have no very great military knowledge myself and I have always had a great respect for that of non-commissioned officers, so I obeyed at once and went down again into my muddy hole, and it was just as well I did, for a split second—or so it seemed —later the searchlight swept over us. The thought occurred to me that although I had organized a whole escape conspiracy, when it came to the point I hadn't had enough common sense to keep myself out of muddy puddles or keep my head down out of the way of searchlights. However, whatever my abilities as a conspirator, the escape had gone off satisfactorily so far. The N.C.O. who had taken command now ordered us to go forward over the field on hands and knees. With a sigh I obeyed, consoling myself with the thought of the wonderful spaghetti that lay ahead.

We had arranged to get into the pine woods beyond the road to which we were now crawling and from there to get down to the beach along which we were to make our way into Rimini. That was as far as our plans went. After that we just hoped for the best. But for the moment we went forward on hands and knees over the clay soil. My companions were much better at this sort of thing than I was and they were well on ahead, but I made progress, cursing to myself about the necessity of ruining my lovely English raincoat. By the time I got to the road the other three were already across it and waiting for me impatiently on the other side. It was then that I saw the dog. It was a great police dog from the camp. Unfortunately it saw me too and it came towards me with hair bristling and ears cocked.

'All up!' I thought. 'We nearly did it.' But as the dog came up I noticed that its tail was wagging. Hurriedly I called on all I had ever read or heard in connection with police dogs, watch dogs and the like and I decided that the thing to do was to remain motionless and see what happened. What actually happened was that the dog approached eagerly, waving its rudder cheerfully, and sat down in front of me in the road looking at me soulfully. It seemed glad to meet a human being. There was no doubt about its identity. I could see the big collar and the metal disc of the camp dogs now.

I began to talk to it softly in a variety of languages: Italian, French, English and German, but it didn't seem to understand any of them. Polish was probably the thing. Then it got up, came closer and lay down beside me near enough for me to to stroke it: "Good doggie! Good doggie!" It grew even friendlier until finally I got up slowly, fearing that when I moved it would object, but no: it just got up too and accompanied me across the road to join the others, and it was quite obvious that it intended to stay with us. Still being very friendly, for you don't show impatience with a dog that size, I beseeched it in all the four languages I knew to go back to its masters and in the end it understood. Dropping its ears and tail it turned round and went off in the direction of the camp. It was a nice dog—but I breathed a sigh of relief. My three companions were so delighted that they began to sing at the tops of their voices as we tramped off to Rimini.

This I found a bit too much. Who had initiated this whole thing? I had. And who therefore ought to be in charge? Why, I ought. And I remembered their unsympathetic laughter when I fell into the puddle. I determined to assert myself.

"Shut up!" I ordered harshly. "You may have got through the wire, but now we're on the other side and we don't need wire-cutters. You can't speak a word of Italian and Italian's what we need now, so do as I tell you or you've had it."

They were quite bright enough to realize the truth of this and they shut up and followed me. I stalked ahead proudly, my leadership re-established. My pride didn't last long.

I saw him and his machine-pistol just as he shouted "Halt!"
It was an officer with a patrol of half a dozen men. We halted
obediently and they came forward towards us. I heard a groan
behind me. It sounded like the comment of the N.C.O. on my
leadership.

It didn't take the officer long to sum up the situation. From
the band round his arm I could see that he was a member of
the Polish Legion in American service.

"Don't get up to any funny business," he said. "I can see
plain enough what you are: an escaped German officer. And
those chaps behind you are Germans too. Come along back to
the camp."

"What's the hurry?" I said. I had nothing to lose now. "Perhaps we could talk things over first."

"Why not?" he agreed surprisingly. "It's a nice moonlit night.
We can go for a stroll."

The two of us walked ahead and his men went behind with
the N.C.O's, and having got him in a receptive mood I began
to tell him about my meeting with Colonel Beck, the Polish
Foreign Minister, and his wife at a reception given in Taormina
to Himmler and his wife. The Polish officer listented to my
story with great interest. The reception was given at the San-
Domingo Palace Hotel. Madame Beck wore a long dark evening
dress and Himmler's wife wore a flowered crinoline sort of thing.
I had been deeply struck by the contrast in fashions. In honour
of his German guests Beck had arranged for a recital of Chopin.
Himmler's comment when it was all over was: "As long as you
Poles waste your time on Chopin you'll never get anywhere."

The Pole was as indignant about it as I was and I had all I
could do to persuade him of my indignation, for fear he might
take us back to camp after all. I praised Chopin enthusiastically
and assured him of my regard and friendship for the Polish
Republic. I also declared that I thought the Allies had left the
Poles shamelessly in the lurch, and with that I had struck the
right note. The Pole couldn't have agreed more. It was a very
sore point in the relationship between the Poles and their allies.
In the end he gave me a packet of cigarettes and wished me
God-speed. In the meantime my N.C.O's seemed to have established friendship on a somewhat similar basis with the other

Poles. They too had their pockets full of cigarettes, and greatly relieved, and freed of police dogs and Polish guards, we marched off in the growing light of dawn towards Rimini.

The station at Rimini was already crowded and no one took any notice of us. In the restaurant I managed to eat more spaghetti with tomato sauce and ham than I would have thought at all possible. After the many months of pease-pudding our capacities were enormous, and we had quite enough Italian money with us to allow us to feed till we just couldn't eat another thing. After that I left the others in the crowded waiting-room and went off to inquire about the trains. "Inquire about the trains" sounds very fine, but actually they were very few and far between. One train would have satisfied me—in the right direction. Actually I had to be satisfied for the time being with a sort of porter.

He was a little man with a hanging moustache and I planted myself in front of him, relying on my British military rain-coat for effect, and demanded firmly:

"When does the next train leave?"

But my rain-coat—it was in pretty poor condition by this time anyway—failed to impress. The man looked as though he couldn't care less.

"There isn't any train," he said shortly.

I gave him some cigarettes. That was much better.

"In about ten minutes there's a train with Badoglio leave men going to Bologna," he said.

That, I decided, was better than nothing and I went back to the waiting-room to collect the others. They were sitting on the floor singing quietly to themselves. They were singing quietly not from prudence but because they were too full to exert themselves. I got them to their feet and shoo'ed them ahead of me out onto the platform where the train was expected, telling them to board it at once and keep their mouths shut once they were in. I was once again the leader; the man who gave orders.

We got into the train all right and squatted down in the carriage with the Badoglio soldiers, but it wasn't long before, amidst roars of laughter, they told us that you could see a mile off who we were—escaped Germans. Once again I felt a little deflated, but it turned out all right. The Italians didn't seem to care what we were and they shared their wine with us with the greatest amiability. After that the Italians sang their songs and my fellows sang theirs and everybody enjoyed himself. Except me, and I was wondering what the devil we were going to do when we got to Bologna.

Towards morning the train rolled into Bologna station and everyone piled out onto the platform. The first thought of my three companions was more food, but I took command:

"Put it out of your minds," I declared firmly. "We've got to get out of here quick. Come on!"

But they refused to budge. They were hungry. My orders didn't work. I could have left them to it of course and gone off on my own, which would have been safer for me but fatal for them. The thought of the puddle and their laughter almost made me do it, but then I thought of the wire-cutters and forgave them. After all, hunger is a great incentive. So I set myself out to persuade them, informing them that Bologna was in Communist hands and that if the Communists got hold of them they'd have nothing to laugh at—and certainly no macaroni. The only thing for us to do was to get out of town to the north and hope to get a lift to Milan, where I had friends. In the end they allowed themselves to be persuaded and followed me with empty bellies through and out of the town to the north where we parked ourselves by the side of the road and waited. We had had the equivalent of about a hundred marks, but we had spent thirty of them on spaghetti and tomato sauce, so we now had seventy.

One of our number was told off to thumb every car that came along, but very few came and those that did took no notice of him. But then an enormous Negro in a jeep came along, driving from one side of the road to the other whilst we hopped around like rabbits and waved. In the end he consented to stop and we went towards him hopefully. He grinned at us, showing an enormous mouthful of white teeth. He also realized at once who we were. We were in civilian clothing, but perhaps all German fugitives looked the same. He immediately addressed us in broken German.

"Where you going?" he demanded, and at the same time he turned the barrel of his machine-pistol towards us. As I had insisted on taking the leadership my N.C.O.s kept prudently to the rear and left me to it.

"We want to go to Milan," I said.

The Negro looked me up and down and instinctively I stuck my hand into my pocket and produced a bundle of lira notes. The Negro took them wordlessly and put them away in his uniform pocket.

"You know Milan?" he demanded.

"Sure," I declared. "Sure I know Milan."

He then levelled his pistol at my chest whilst behind me my companions disappeared into a near-by ditch.

"I want a woman," he said. "Girls. Can you find me any girls?"

"Of course!" I exclaimed confidently. "Girls galore in Milan. I'll find 'em for you."

"Get in then."

At that we all piled into the jeep and he drove off like mad, racing through traffic and pedestrians that it was a marvel that he hit nothing. In the meantime behind us my three companions, their good humour and optimism thoroughly restored, bellowed German soldiers' songs. In the meantime I sat beside the Negro and wondered how on earth I could provide him with girls. Then I thought of "The Italian Provinces" brothel in Milan, so called because each of its inmates was known by the name of one of the Italian provinces. There was "Rome" with her generous curves. She did duty for N.C.O.s. Then there was "Naples" with her fiery eyes. She was meat for the officers. And so on. Yes, that was the place. I couldn't think of anywhere else which could provide so much of the necessary at short notice.

Shortly before we came to Milan the Negro stopped the jeep, sprang out, drew his pistol and levelled it at us.

"I shoot you all kaputt," he screamed in occupation German, and his pistol barrel wandered from one true German heart to the next and back again. He looked to me like a one-man execution squad just about to go into action. "I shoot you all dead if you don't find me girls," he added more hopefully.

"But of course I'll find you girls," I said soothingly. "No doubt about it. Just jump back in and drive on. I'll show you the way."

46

Fortunately he too allowed himself to be persuaded and he calmed down and climbed back into the jeep. I then directed him to the rather shabby quarter of Milan in which "The Italian Provinces" was situated. The place itself was decrepit too and I think the Negro was beginning to think we were going to entice him somewhere and murder him on the quiet, but then the sound of women's voices restored his confidence.

In the meantime my three companions had entered thoroughly into the spirit of the thing. They too thought the idea of a woman highly attractive. Since the previous May they hadn't had a chance. Now they were all agog and the dirty stories were flying. One of the N.C.O.s was just describing his girl friend's legs when I stopped the Negro outside the place.

They all sprang out and rushed into the house like ravening wolves, though my men had no money any more. The first woman they came across was old and wrinkled, much to their disappointment. She was the brothel mistress. A cat was sitting on her shoulder. Fortunately she was in no doubt as to our requirements and she began to clap her hands and shout her version of "Shop!"

At that the girls came running: "Naples", "Toscano" and the rest, with flashing eyes and waggling hips, looking keenly for a suitable partner. The Negro appropriately produced our bundle of lira notes and the old woman's watery eyes glistened approvingly and she clapped and shouted louder than ever. The Negro now began to distribute chocolate and biscuits from his capacious pockets, and whilst one after the other my companions disappeared upstairs I took the old woman aside, gave her what money I had left and asked her to do her best to keep them all amused, which she willingly promised to do. Whether she did so or not I never had occasion to discover, but I felt that I had done my duty by them all, the Negro included, and now I left them to their own devices. I did subsequently discover that all three of my companions arrived home safely in the end.

With a clear conscience I left "The Italian Provinces" and walked round in the streets for a while. Near the cathedral I came across one of those Italian establishments where you can not only have a bath, but also have your clothes cleaned, your shoes polished, your hair cut, your nails manicured and so on.

Suddenly I felt that a bath was the one thing in all the world I wanted. Carefully I searched through all my pockets and managed to rake together enough money for the purpose. When I had taken a bath and my clothes had been cleaned up and my shoes polished I felt the need for a little luxury, a manicure. I made my way to the manicure department and it felt expansively like old times. There I found a gentle-faced girl sitting beside her manicure table and waiting for the next customer. I sat down and as she started to attend to me I remembered who she was. Her face had seemed familiar. Her name was Isabella and she came from Rome, where she had attended to me—not only in the saloon. We knew each other very well. When she looked up from my hands she recognized me:

"Eugenio!" she exclaimed.

It strikes me as unnecessary to describe the further course or nature of our relationship. Sufficient to say that I stayed with one of her friends for three days, ate well, drank well and amused myself very agreeably. I had almost forgotten that I was a fugitive from Rimini.

On December 24th when Isabella was decorating a Christmas tree in my honour I suddenly felt a need to go to church, not merely to give thanks for my successful escape. I pushed my way through the crowds of worshippers into the cathedral. It is an enormous building of brick cased in marble, the third largest church in Europe, and its elaborate Gothic design always reminds me of a fine lace tablecloth. I remembered the last time I had been in church; it was at a High Mass solemnized by the Pope himself in St. Peter's. I had been in the front row then not far from the Pope under his gold and silver baldachin. But now I stood there in a dirty British rain-coat and the little Cardinal who was saying Mass appeared to me even more holy than the Pope himself. Quite moved I stood against one of the great pillars with their canopied niches and around me was the murmur of hundreds of the faithful at their prayers. Now and again there was the tinkle of the server's bell.

The little cardinal went up to the altar. I knew him quite well. His name was Schuster. He always reminded me of a delicate alabaster statue. He stood there now and preached a sermon and his voice sounded impressive and powerful in the vast and overwhelming interior.

"Come unto me all ye that labour and are heavy laden . . ."

Maybe I didn't labour but I was heavy laden. 'Right, Your Eminence' I thought. 'You can have that!' And I remembered the subterranean passage that led from the cathedral to the Archbishop's Palace on the other side of the street. In other days I had been taken through it by one of the Cardinal's Monsignori. Beneath the crypt was the small doorway which opened onto this passage. Whilst the congregation knelt and prayed I quietly left my pillar, went to the door, opened it and went down into the passage, which was lighted by candles.

I went forward under one of the main streets of Milan and my footsteps echoed in the narrow corridor. A spot or two of water fell from the roof onto my rain-coat. The Cardinal's sermon seemed to give this long solemn walk through the bowels of the earth its justification. In the Archbishop's Palace I announced myself to one of the Monsignori. He came to meet me through the door of one of the magnificent rooms I knew from former times and when he spoke he had much the same gentle, almost childlike voice as the Cardinal himself.

"What do you wish?"

"I am Eugen Dollmann."

He took a closer look at me and his astonished eyes ran over my rain-coat. Despite the mud and the clay it was still clearly a British officer's coat.

"You have changed sides very rapidly, Signor Dollmann," he observed finally.

I had expected something of the sort.

"Not at all," I said, "but be good enough to announce me to His Eminence."

The Monsignor bowed and led me into one of the great reception rooms where he presented me in accordance with the usual custom with a glass of rose liqueur.

I looked at the long-stemmed glass with the light rose-coloured liquid and I remembered Mussolini. The day before the end Mussolini was in this very palace to discuss the last chances of survival with the Cardinal. He too had been served with this liqueur. Twenty-four hours later he was dead.

"Tell me, Monsignor," I said to the little man with the delicate features who had placed the glass in front of me, "do you think that it will have the same sequel for me as for Mussolini?"

He smiled for the first time.

"I don't think so," he replied. "Besides, Mussolini did not drink it."

I laughed and thus encouraged I took up the little glass and drank.

At that moment the Cardinal entered the room.

CHAPTER III

ASYLUM WITH ORANGE BLOSSOM

OR a moment he stopped at the door of the room and looked at me. His small, delicate hand made a sign and the Monsignor left us together: the fugitive in the British officer's raincoat and the Milan Cardinal in his purple cassock. He stood there, expectantly it seemed to me, and I hoped he was still in the "Come unto me" mood.

I went towards him, made the indication of a bow, for I feared that the very worn knees of my trousers, which had suffered a good deal whilst I was crawling over the ploughed field to freedom, would show and I kissed his amethyst ring.

"Your Eminence," I said.

Then he recognized me.

"*Oh, é Lei,* Dollmann!" he exclaimed, and his voice would have been more at home in a quiet study than in this enormous room.

"Yes," I said. "I am Eugen Dollmann," and my voice sounded loud and harsh to my ears. He glanced at the empty liqueur glass and smiled. I wondered whether he recalled the fate of Mussolini, but then I remembered why I had come and the text of his Christmas sermon. I pulled myself together and muttered something about his help. His hand indicated a chair and I sat down and whilst my lips almost automatically poured out the story of my escape I had plenty of opportunity to study the Cardinal's reactions. He sat there quietly opposite me and listened patiently to what I had to say. And I remembered a time—not so long ago—when he had been far from quiet and peaceful. Then he had been a vigorous fighter, doing everything in his power to save Upper Italy from destruction.

He was one of the three men to whom Florence, Bologna, Milan and the whole of the Po plateau owed their salvation. It

51

wasn't the Neo-Fascists, or the Partisans, or the steadily retreating German troops who bothered themselves about the preservation of an ancient culture, but the cardinals of the Church, Schuster of Milan, Dalla Costa of Florence, and Nasalli-Recchi of Bologna, and it was they who persuaded the German High Command to spare the Po district.

Cardinal Schuster sent Captain Ghisetti to me in my villa. It was at the time when the German forces were preparing to fight for Upper Italy. Hitler's scorched-earth tactic was to be applied here too. Ghisetti gave me no peace. He was in my villa every day, a very un-Italian and unemotional member of the Italian Secret Service. Every day he had new memoranda and dossiers in his brief-case. He was a man of very few words and he let the documents speak for themselves. And there were cogent appeals from Cardinal Schuster to the German High Command imploring them to spare the countryside.

"Discuss the matter with Kesselring," was about all Ghisetti ever had to say, but he brought me one memorandum after the other from the Cardinal. I went to Kesselring and he read what the Cardinal had to say. In the end Upper Italy was evacuated without being destroyed.

And now Schuster sat opposite me as though nothing of the sort had ever been true, or as though it had been something so natural and matter of course that he would have done it every day. In fact I believe he would have done it every day if necessary.

I remembered another scene. This time the leading actor was Cardinal dalla Costa, a modern Savanarola, sinewy and ascetic, an enemy of all luxury and pomp. The subterranean hall into which I was ushered was lit by torches in sconces fixed on the marble walls. It was all very romantic, like a shot from a Renaissance film, but it struck me as an incongruous background for the business we had in hand. The German troops were about to evacuate Florence, but before doing so they intended to destroy "all points of strategic importance". That meant the lovely bridges of Florence for one thing—and many other things too. Florence was full of them.

Dalla Costa stood opposite me:

"I have asked you to come here, Signor Dollmann, because I want to implore you to leave Florence without first laying the city in dust and ashes."

He was dressed in a brown cloak with a hood which was over his head. In its shadow his dark brown eyes gleamed fiercely. It was not difficult to think of Savanarola. From Cardinal dalla Costa I went straight to Kesselring and told him what the Cardinal had said. Only one historical bridge was destroyed when the German troops pulled out. Everything else—with one or two rare exceptions—was spared.

The third of these men was Cardinal Nasalli-Recchi of Bologna.

"Listen, Signor Dollmann," he said to me with a smile. "What soldier would continue following a leader who could promise him nothing but defeat and never a victory? And now I need a victory, Signor Dollmann, and it would not be to your disadvantage."

He smiled a good deal, this corpulent, good-humoured Prince of the Church. But because he smiled it did not mean that he was not deadly in earnest. He was begging us for a favour now, but he was not a man who needed to beg. He had power and authority. Even the Communists respected him, and Bologna was the stronghold of Italian Communism, a dangerous centre of the Italian Resistance.

At the time Gauleiter Sauckel was in Bologna in connection with the "recruiting" of labour power for Germany. To this end he had ordered a mass raid which was to take place in Bologna that very night in order to press-gang every able-bodied citizen of Bologna between the ages of eighteen and forty-five and deport him to Germany for forced labour.

The Cardinal, who maintained relations both with us and with the Resistance, knew all about Sauckel's plan and he was anxious to prevent it at all costs.

"And now it's up to you," he said with a smile as we shook hands. "I need this victory. Talk to Marshal Kesselring about it."

And then, almost as though it were an afterthought, the short, plump, good-humoured prelate added: "You never know, I might be able to prevent the Partisans from attacking you in the rear." And he went on smiling amiably and I smiled back.

I spoke to Marshal Kesselring and the raids never took place. The Cardinal had his victory and the able-bodied men of Bologna slept peacefully in their beds that night—and when we pulled out our rear was secure.

Cardinal Schuster had listened without interruption to my story. It had taken me into his palace now and I was repeating my request for assistance. When I think back on it it must have sounded more like a demand than a request: "The time has come for you to help me now, Your Eminence." The situation was too urgent for finesse.

Cardinal Schuster smiled rarely. He was polite, but cool and subtle, but above all he was objective. He never showed enthusiasm or emotion. He was not the type. I must say that I was not feeling very enthusiastic myself. He was walking up and down in thought now and I watched him as his small, pointed patent leather shoes moved in and out under his cassock. For no particular reason I thought of Major Bridge's rain-coat. The Cardinal's secretary had taken me for a British officer at first. Perhaps there was a possibility of getting away with that? The Cardinal spoke at last:

"I can offer you two possibilities," he said. It was as matter of fact as though a salesman were offering me two kinds of material.

"You could go into a Jesuit house where you would enjoy all ordinary civic liberties."

He smiled a little and I waited.

"But you wouldn't be able to get out again. At least not for the time being. On the other hand you could seek the protection of the Cardinal Ferrari Institute, which is under my personal patronage and which looks after narcotic cases and the like. There you would be able to get out."

The salesman waited with his two samples spread out for my choice.

"I have met only one drug addict in my life, Your Eminence," I said finally, "and that was Goering, but I'm quite prepared to extend my education."

Cardinal Schuster smiled again.

54

"It won't be as bad as all that, Signor Dollmann," he said quietly, and I thought from the tone of his voice that he was telling the truth. "Some of the patients there are recovering from various forms of neurosis and have never been drug addicts."

I was just about to say that I had seen a great deal more of hysteria and neurosis than I had of drug addicts when I heard the click of the door and I half turned, being unwilling to turn my back on a man powerful enough to bring me into a discreet lunatic asylum where I should be safe from political interrogations.

The door opened and Monsignor X came in. He was a tall and active man who looked as though he were not averse from the creature comforts of this world. We had met before. He had also played his role in the behind-the-scenes negotiations concerning the fate of Upper Italy. He was also the chief editor of the Catholic newspaper *Italia,* but that by no means exhausted his many activities. He was also a very capable business man and financier in the uniform of the Church and he managed the business affairs of the Curia. He did it extraordinarily well, too. With a keen business sense and a knowledge of all the tricks of the trade he made it possible for the Curia to meet all its charitable obligations. At the same time he would write moving articles in his newspaper about the social conscience of the Church. This admirable circle of activities kept him eternally busy, greatly assisted the Church, and did no one any harm. If he had not been a priest, Monsignor could have been a business tycoon.

He greeted the Cardinal with deep respect, and then he greeted me with a good deal less, after which he listened to the whole story.

"Ah, that's wonderful!" he exclaimed when he heard of my decision. Now although I realized its necessity I should hardly have described it as wonderful, but I made no comment.

"Wonderful!" he repeated. "To-morrow I have to go out there myself. One or two articles to write for *Italia,* you know. And then, whilst I am out there, I should like to write one or two things about our more recent past, and in that respect you could certainly assist me."

He then talked for a while in a low tone to the Cardinal, and when he had finished he took his leave respectfully. At the door he turned back to me.

"I am glad we are in agreement, Signor Dollman. I will look after you.

And that was that. At least it meant that there need be no worry about my immediate future; with such powerful patronage nothing much could go wrong.

The next visitor was Captain Ghisetti. He never either opened or closed a door quietly, and he didn't this time. Cardinal Schuster was obviously used to his little ways and he ignored the noise. Ghisetti stalked towards us. He was a tall man and he stooped a little. It was obviously the thing for him to wear spurs and you missed them at once. He was a rather morose but not at all a disagreeable man, and I quite liked him. When he greeted me I even thought I detected a flicker of pleasure in his large, dark eyes, though it really seemed unlikely that he ever felt any emotion at all. He shook hands with me in a matter-of-fact way as though we had parted only yesterday, and then he too listened to what I had to say. When I had finished he observed in that deep, base voice of his that didn't in the least suit his appearance:

"So now the Church is to have an opportunity to repay you for your good offices then."

For a moment my ego began to swell up inside me again, which was a pleasant change, but then he added:

"Though, naturally, what you did was a matter of course."

And there I was again, back in my role of suppliant. How often third parties butted in to deprive me of my halo by some totally superfluous observation of that sort! It annoyed me a little, but I said nothing. I was not in a position to be fussy, and Ghisetti was the man who was going to take me out to my lunatic asylum.

Early next day there was a car waiting outside. It had a long black body and it bore a depressing similarity to the official hearse of the President of the German Republic. However, I climbed into it with a good heart and sat in front between Captain Ghisetti, who was at the wheel, and Monsignor X., and we drove off and out into the lovely countryside of Lombardy.

It was a cold December day and the landscape was bare. In the distance mountains rose into the sky, and over everything there was an almost uncanny atmosphere of peace and quiet. Where maize grew in profusion in the summer months the fields were empty and frozen hard. From the distant mountains small white clouds rose into the clear morning sky. The trees lining the road, and the poplars farther into the countryside, were leafless, standing out as stark skeletons against the sky. Although it was winter I thought I had never seen the country looking so beautiful as it did on that December day.

At the end of our drive we stopped in front of a pleasant two-storied house with walls of mellowed ochre. Its windows reached right down to the ground so that you could look into the ground-floor rooms. Behind the windows there seemed to be a sort of conservatory, and I could see blooming roses, and here and there even an orchid. It all looked very agreeable and it struck me that the drug addicts were doing quite well for themselves. The garden itself was beautiful too, but it had been allowed to grow a little wild.

A young woman who was carrying a large bunch of keys came down the broad stone flags from the house towards us. To my surprise she made a constant rattling noise with her keys; I had always thought that neurotics needed peace and quiet. She was a slim young woman with doe-like eyes.

"A new patient for us?" she asked when she came up.

I shook my head and was about to explain to her light-heartedly that my trouble was of a very different nature when Ghisetti, usually so silent, found his voice to interrupt me:

"Yes, a new patient for you," he declared firmly. "He isn't really very ill, but he also isn't very well. A border-line case, you understand."

Observing me about to protest, Monsignor X. put his hand on my shoulder warningly and took up the conversation:

"Above all he needs quiet. He has gone through a good deal, you understand."

"Of course," said the young woman, who turned out to be the daughter of the head of the sanatorium.

My two companions then left me to the girl who took me to my room. Once again the place seemed very little like what

I had imagined an asylum for drug addicts to be. The room was more like a room in a normal hotel. There was a bed, two chairs and a chest of drawers that might have stood in a hotel in Milan—or Berlin. There was nothing out of the ordinary in the room at all—except perhaps the vase of beautiful flowers in the window.

I first met the two old ladies at dinner that evening. As I learned later, they had been put there fifteen years previously by their family, which since then had had nothing whatever to do with them apart from paying the bill regularly, but all the time they were expecting a visit from some of their relatives. The visit never took place and the hope had now hardened into an obsession.

They were at least eighty years old and they sat at a table of their own at a little distance from the other inmates. Beside them on the table was a railway time-table and this they constantly consulted. During the meal one or other of them was always at the window, from which the entrance to the small branch railway station of the place could be seen. If a train happened to come in the one on the watch would shout: "They're coming now! They're coming now!" Whereupon the other one would leap up, usually upsetting her soup or her dinner plate, and rush over to the window to look out too. The two of them would then excitedly study the few travellers who had come with the train, but who always disappeared elsewhere.

The two naturally had photographs of their expected relatives and they knew their appearance in such detail that at any time they could have dictated a police "Wanted" notice. But every day they had to suffer the same disappointment: no one ever came to see them. Every time this happened they would go back to their places and sit down heavily at the disordered table, stained with soup or bespattered with the remains of their food, staring at nothing, ignoring their wet skirts and digesting their disappointment. Then suddenly one of them would sieze the time-table and together they would begin to pore over it to discover when the next train arrived, shouting all the time: "They'll be on the next train! They'll be on the next train!" And each would try to outdo the other in assurances that "of course" it was the next train they would come on.

When I first witnessed this pathetic and yet disturbing performance I was so shattered that I almost decided to abandon
the sanatorium and make straight for the railway station myself,
but for one thing that would have been very dangerous, and
for another the doe-eyed maiden gave me a feeling not only
that I would be safe under her roof but also that I should
experience more comforting things than the behaviour of the
two touched old ladies. For half an hour or so (not longer, to
tell the truth) I felt terrible, but then I made up my mind to it.
After all, it was a sanatorium and you had to expect such things
and no one else seemed to take any notice of it. Then I went out
into the park in search of peace and fresh air.

Another inmate of the place was a little man, still dark-haired,
but worn and pale like all, or almost all, big business men whose
life consists largely of narcotics, women and high-pressure
affairs. He was old enough to have got over everything except
the narcotics—that was why he was here. He was a quite
intelligent man and his hobby-horse was the need for the in-
corporation of the West into the East and the establishment
of an empire in which a good many furs would be worn. He
had been a big fur dealer and he had done a good deal of business with Eastern Europe. He had a soft spot in his heart for
Siberia, and although the basis of it was commercial it was
concealed under a mask of humanitarianism and a love of peace.
On the little finger of his right hand he wore a magnificent
diamond ring which dated from the days of his great prosperity
and which he now flourished under everyone's nose.

He was still prosperous enough to be able to afford a six
months stay in a sanatorium from time to time to cure him
of his addiction. After that, hoping against hope that he was
cured, he would return to his normal life—and start all over
again with his heroin. The great desire for the drug would
overcome him at about five o'clock in the afternoon and then
he would leave his secretary and his partner, who arrived every
morning at the sanatorium, and begin to tramp up and down
miserably like a trapped silver fox (to keep the picture to his
furs), ignoring the other's remarks. Finally he would leave the
room and rush upstairs to the duty sister and beg for "just a
little injection" to soothe his nerves, and she would then give

him an injection of something he believed to be heroin. This performance was repeated daily in exactly the same fashion at exactly the same time. No doubt he was the soul of punctuality in business and all other affairs.

Then there was an Italian Duchess named Antonietta. From a distance she was still a very beautiful woman, but her youth had gone and she spent her life striving desperately to extend it by every means in her power including innumerable plastic operations. She must have been fabulously rich, for every day the leading fashion houses sent her new dresses to try on, whilst masseuses, manicurists, chiropodists and other cosmetic specialists surrounded her with their attentions. She had lived the life of so many other rich, aristocratic women, spending her time at cocktail parties, receptions, the theatre, the opera and so on, and the rest of it in preparing herself for them.

She was still bombarded with invitations of all kinds and at lunch she would entertain her fellow-guests by explaining what they were and who they were from, with digressions concerning their characters and weaknesses. After that she would go up to her room to prepare herself to go to the one or other of these functions. At five o'clock her black Cadillac would drive up and down she would come, escorted by her maid, descending the main staircase in a magnificent evening dress, her much lifted face made up for the evening. But then just before reaching the door she would appear to remember something—she had already seemed a little upset—then suddenly she would turn about and run back to her room, her maid chasing after her. About half an hour later the maid would come down again and dismiss the chauffeur. The Cadillac would drive up every day at the same time, and drive away without its mistress a little later.

Another inmate was a distinguished Italian general, who spent his time defeating Badoglio, the "Southerner", and the decadent Allies on his maps. He was a tall, lean man with a mane of white hair and bushy white eyebrows and his room in the sanatorium was like an army staff-room. Enormous but ancient ordnance maps hung on the walls, decorated with little flags on pins, and on his table were dividers, rulers, pencils, slide-rules and other instruments of theoretical battle. Striding up and down with heavy steps that made his mop of white hair wobble, he would declare in a loud voice that once again Badoglio, the hound, had fallen victim to his brilliant strategy. After that he would mobilise as many of his fellow inmates as he could, almost dragging them to his maps, and explaining to them at length how the battle went that destroyed both Badoglio and the Allies, manipulating little pieces of wood of different shapes and sizes representing divisions, armoured units and so on, and ignoring the yawns of his bored listeners. There was also a match-stick which he moved hurriedly here and there.

"That, gentlemen," he would explain, "is the Duce himself, who is also taking part in the battle."

He usually managed to get the business over by the late afternoon, but now and again the Duce was still in the midst of the undecided battle when the supreme war lord felt the need for heroin. After that he didn't care what happened to the Allies, Badoglio or the Duce, and the whole of Italy could have been laid waste.

The lovely Marina was an Italian film star. She was perhaps thirty at the time and she was adored and sought after by all Italy's film producers. But Marina was an inmate of our sanatorium. However, that did not prevent them from coming to her when they had a new film in mind to persuade her to accept the leading role. The only condition Marina always made was that she was to wear nothing but dresses with long sleeves. There was a good reason for this. Her forearms were pitted with the marks of heroin injections and the merciless glass eye of the cine-camera would never have missed them.

One day her anxious and despairing producers once again found a suitable role for her. It was as Josephine and she was to visit Bonaparte, Emperor-to-be, in Milan. The film people did their utmost to make it all historically accurate; a set of eighteenth-century Milan was built up, local villagers were dressed up in revolutionary uniforms—and I must say they looked the part—and the people, all in suitable rags, were there to cheer the pair. The lights were on, the cameras were whirring and Napoleon advanced to the spot where Josephine was to meet him and give him the kiss of welcome whilst the troops presented arms and the crowds cheered. But no Josephine appeared. She was in her costume all right, but she was lying on her bed in her room with her sleeve rolled up giving herself an injection of heroin. And once again all the preparations were ruined. Napoleon ran around in despair followed by the director wringing his hands and both of them wailing out loud. In the end everything was packed up and the whole party returned in despair to Milan and peace descended on our park once again —whilst in her room Marina lay half in coma, still in the long-sleeved dress she was to wear for her part.

But we didn't always live in a fantasy world of Duchesses, rich fur merchants and film stars. Reality stalked on the scene one beautiful spring morning in the shape of twelve former Partisans. The Italian Government had sent them to our sanatorium to recuperate and they were quartered in a special wing of the house. There was nothing remarkable about them and after a while none of us paid any attention to them. At first I had regarded them with distrust and I continued to keep out of their way as far as possible, but it was now spring and we all went for walks amidst the blossoming plants in our park and so did they.

One day on one of these walks I was suddenly accosted by one of them who fell on his knees before me and began to kiss my hand. I thought he had gone mad and did my best to free myself from his embarrassing attentions, but in vain.

"Signor Colonello!" he raved. "How grateful we are to you."

In the meantime I was trying to make some sense out of the scene and wondering whether his lunatic gratitude might at any moment turn to fury.

"What's it all about?" I demanded. "I'm not a colonel. I've never seen you in my life before."

"Oh, yes, Signor Colonello! Oh, yes! Don't you remember? You saved my life. In the cellars of Reggio Emilia. Don't you remember now?"

Something dawned on me and I had a closer look at him. Then the whole business returned to me. It was in December 1944 in a torture hole of the Neo-Fascists.

One night the Bishop of Reggio came to my apartment and dragged me out with the words: "You must come at once, Signor Dollmann, or they'll murder them all." And he hurried me through the streets to the torture cellars of the Reggio Emilia. When we opened the door I thought someone must be frying sausages although the smell was a little strange. I made some would-be humorous remark to the good bishop but all he would say was "Come on, come quickly". I followed him obediently. What I saw was not altogether an uncommon sight during the Italian fratricidal war.

A number of naked men were strapped to tables and their torturers were gathered round them in glee brandishing hot irons. The man who now knelt before me was strapped to a table shrieking horribly. Part of his flesh was already charred and they were about to apply the torture again. When we burst in on them they looked round with sadistic fury in their eyes. I had two hefty Non-Coms with me and I made them a sign; there was no need for words. They willingly pitched into the thwarted Neo-Fascists, bundling them roughly to one side, and then they released the groaning Partisans from the tables. The victims were hurried off in ambulances to a German military hospital where, at my request, Kesselring's own doctor attended to them.

After that I thought no more either of the Partisan victims or their Neo-Fascist torturers. In any case, I knew very well that this torturing business was not altogether one-sided: it might easily have been the other way round. However, here was one of the men I had saved, now on his knees and kissing my hand in gratitude.

After that I lived like a prince, and a good deal of my time was spent with the Partisans in their quarters, eating roast chicken and roast goose, which they received from home and had specially cooked for them. As far as the Partisans were concerned I was now probably the most popular German Colonel in Italy, and I began to put on weight. Whilst I spent my time between lovely walks amidst the blossoming trees and bushes in the park and eating enormous meals with the Partisans, the rest of the sanatorium was divided into two hostile parts over the military question.

Unfortunately our general was no longer able to fight his battles undisturbed. We had a new arrival, a "Badoglio" colonel, who belonged to the other camp. Even physically he was the exact opposite of the general, being short, agile and bespectacled. In fact he looked more like a university professor than a soldier.

As soon as the general began to announce his renewed victory over the hound Badoglio, the colonel would bob up squeaking in his high-pitched voice: "That's all nonsense. He's really lost the battle. He's always lost every battle." And his fattish face would shine with malicious glee. "We won," he would say. "We won. We were the real victors." And before the irate general could do anything about it he would run off and lock himself in the billiards room.

Before long the sanatorium was in an uproar over the squabbles of the two, but by five o'clock everything was peaceable again, for this was the hour that Mirella, the girl with the doe-like eyes, had fixed for her daily intervention. She could do anything with them merely by promising injections of their favourite drugs, and the promise was enough to reconcile the two camps and get them drinking vermouth together united in a common affection for her—though she never kept her promises.

Needless to say, I felt myself somewhat out of place in this bedlam and instead of walking in the lovely park I often went into Milan instead, where I spent many hours in cafés and bars and sought to forget the sanatorium and its inmates by drowning the memory in strong drink. Every time I left the house on one of these excursions my departure appeared almost more difficult to me than my escape from Rimini, though there was no barbed-wire here, no watch-towers with machine-guns and no Polish guards with dogs. But my progress to the gates was almost more closely watched. Behind almost every bush was a hopeful lunatic awaiting an opportunity to press a scrap of paper into my hand secretly with the name and address of a doctor or druggist from whom he hoped to obtain supplies of his favourite poison—the very poison he was here to cure himself of.

I could have had the Cadillac of the duchess, the whole military paraphernalia of the general, and a night of love with the film diva if I had only consented to bring back what they wanted, but having happily escaped from the clutches of the Allied military police I had now no desire to fall into the hands of the Italian police as a drug trafficker, and so I did nothing but promise—all the same, I could have used that Cadillac!

One day I was sitting in a café in Milan and wondering what to do with the rest of the day when a well-dressed man came up to my table and bowed.

"Dr. Dollmann I believe?"

'This is it,' I thought. 'Why didn't I stay where I was? I'd have been safe there.' And in my mind I measured the distance to the street and calculated my chances of finding a taxi to carry me away from the attentions of this obvious secret-service agent. But when I stood up to put my intention into effect I recognized him and with relief I sat down again and motioned him to take a seat opposite me. He was a lawyer named Ardinghello whom I had known quite well at one time. He smiled at me now just as he had always smiled at me and it had a soothing effect on my over-heated fugitive's imagination. In my relief I told him the whole story, where I was now and what plans I had for the future. I must say that they were so confused and unconvincing that the lawyer's keen mind must have regarded them as mere inventions perhaps to make myself more interesting for the future. However, he listened patiently and reacted objectively:

"I have some good friends in the Grand Lodge," he said. "Perhaps some of them could do something for you."

I shook my head resignedly. At that moment the suggestion seemed even more unreal than my own. But Ardinghello insisted that his friends would be interested in me and in the end I agreed to go with him that very afternoon and meet one of the high-ups of the Lodge. I had had some idea that I should be ushered straight into a lodge meeting with masked men, mysterious lights and all the usual trimmings, but the room I went into with Ardinghello was more like a laboratory, and there were retorts and glass bottles and tubes on shelves around, together with human skulls, and in glass jars exposed to the fascinated eye of the beholder were human brains. A tall, well-built gentleman rose when we came in and put down an illustrated journal, in which, so he informed us, he had been reading an article on the cerebral functioning of Siamese twins. I knew him to be a well-known psychiatrist.

We discussed my escape and his work politely for a while and then he invited us into another room. There were no brains pickled in alcohol there, but instead a number of the leading Freemasons of Milan, who were waiting for us. They were obviously all well-to-do business men and they all wore suits of Italian cut but English material. They welcomed me in a friendly fashion and then a general discussion took place on a variety of subjects, passing from trade and industry to law and philosophy, and on, for a change, to local problems.

During the course of this conversation it was mentioned casually that they had certain funds at their disposal, which I could well believe, though I was not particularly interested in the fact. I paid more attention to the conversation than it would have deserved in the ordinary way, for I was anxious not to miss anything of interest to me in my present situation, and I knew that sooner or later something would turn up. Then it transpired that these funds could be used to assist me.

"You would of course accept our assistance, Signor Dollmann?"

I was quite prepared to accept anyone's assistance, so why not theirs? Having set their minds at rest on that score I thought it natural to inquire what they would expect of me in return.

"Oh!" exclaimed one of them, as though such considerations were a trifle vulgar, "no doubt you will be writing your memoirs, Herr Doktor?"

"I'm pretty certain to," I agreed. "Once I'm safely out of this."

"But that's just what we want to help you in. Do you need a passport, for example?"

I agreed enthusiastically that, for example, one of the things I needed was certainly a passport.

"We will give you a passport of any country you want, your travelling expenses and a sum of money sufficient to allow you to make your own arrangements when you arrive there."

That sounded too good to be true.

"And all you need do in return is to let us have the copyright in your memoirs together with full editorial liberty. Naturally we should purchase the copyright separately."

So that was it. They wanted to exploit my as yet unwritten memoirs in some way or other as yet unknown to me. However, the thought of the passport and the money was tempting.

" I must have time to think it over," I said.

If those gentlemen should ever read these lines they will have one more reason for knowing that I did think it over—and decided otherwise.

After that Ardinghello and I left the strange house of pickled brains, polished skulls—and funds for the purchase of the as yet unwritten memoirs of ex-colonels of German origin. That evening I returned to the sanatorium in the beautiful park and its blossoming trees and bushes, and from all sides came urgent whispers inquiring about the various drugs I was supposed to have brought back with me. And great was the disappointment when they discovered that I had brought them back nothing at all. As this had happened before, and as it continued to happen, my reputation amongst the inmates of the place gradually declined. Aware of my waning popularity I was therefore quite bucked when one day Mirella of the doe-like eyes informed me rather anxiously that two gentlemen wished to see me.

"I don't altogether like the look of them," she said, "but they insist on speaking to you."

"Well, whoever they are it would be difficult to avoid seeing them. In any case, who knows?"

And with that I marched boldly into the reception room. One look at the two gentlemen I found there waiting for me was quite enough to assure me that whatever they were they were not policemen. They looked to me more like aristocrats who had seen better days, and that is exactly what they proved to be. They were both tall, dark-haired, elegant men. Italian cavalry types I would have said, and again I was right. They both bowed smartly when I came in, and I formally returned the compliment.

"Signor Dollmann," one of them began, "we are officers of the Royal Court . . ."

"And we have a request to make to you," interrupted the other one.

"Herr Doktor," went on the first man. And the only person who said nothing was I. 'If they call me "Herr Doktor", they won't be meaning any harm and they won't have come to arrest me,' I thought. My relationship to the House of Savoy had always been excellent, so, reassured, I sat down comfortably and let them talk.

In the meantime the first man had been talking on and on and he had arrived precisely at my relationship with the Italian Royal House when I started listening to him again.

"You see," he said when he observed that he had caught my attention again, "we know your attitude and we know that you were always friendly to the Royal House . . ."

"That is so," put in the other, "and on one or two occasions you saved the family of the King from very embarrassing situations. And therefore we have come to ask you . . ."

"Well, what is it exactly you've come to ask me?" I said, and apart from the one or two words of greeting at the start it was the first thing I had said. The old relations of my family to the House of Wittelsbach and my own relations to the highest Italian aristocracy came back to me, and it was suddenly as though I had never worn the uniform of the Third Reich and that I had always belonged to these people. It was well known that the House of Savoy had done everything possible to protect Italy from the encroachments of the Nazis and that in this connection I too had done rather more than my superiors had intended me to do. And it was Victor Emmanuel who by his capitulation in September 1943 and by the arrest of Mussolini had saved Italy from the tragic fate of Germany.

My two visitors now repeated all this to me, though quite unnecessarily, for I knew it all only too well from my own experience. When they arrived at the end of their historical reminiscences I repeated my question: "What is it exactly you have come to ask me?"

"We want to ask you," began the first man with the narrow, bony face, "as the historian that you were before . . ."

I coughed significantly.

"Not as a Colonel," he continued, "but as a historian, to write us a memorandum . . ."

I could guess what was coming now.

" . . . on the relationship between the Italian Royal House and the Third Reich."

"Because," put in the other quickly before I could say anything, "on June 6th a referendum is taking place as to whether Italy is to remain a monarchy or become a republic, and . . ."

"I understand," I interrupted, "but you must believe me when I tell you that I will do it willingly . . ."

It was their turn to interrupt:

"The Royal House will never forget your services."

"Perhaps not," I said, "but that's not the point. I wanted to make it quite clear that I would do it very willingly for the Royal House—whether it ever forgets or not."

Two weeks later I went into Milan again. Having written the required memorandum I felt a keen desire to see King Umberto again before the referendum actually took place. Incidentally, their anxiety was quite justified: the upshot was very doubtful. When the King left Milan Cathedral after a service I was amongst the crowds gathered in the square to greet him. Some people were cheering, but others were booing and even throwing stones. On leaving the Cathedral the King sought the protection of the Archbishop's Palace as I had done five months previously before leaving for my discreet lunatic asylum. I had a very strong feeling that banishment was the fate that was awaiting the tall, pale King who walked quickly, dressed in civilian clothes, through the mingled shouts of *"Evviva!"* and *"Abasse!"* being shrieked by those who were as yet still his subjects.

On my return to the sanatorium, now filled with the scent of blossom in addition to its cracked old ladies, its deranged Generals and its drug-addicted Duchesses and film divas, I felt so upset that I decided to seek solace and refuge in a dose of heroin myself. It was very nice weather for the experiment. It was pouring in torrents and the heavily perfumed air of the place seemed unable to escape into the open. The atmosphere was so oppressive that it almost drove me out of my mind. The referendum on the fate of the monarchy had taken place that day. In desperation I approached the film diva and secured a dose of snow from her.

In my room I sniffed it up my nose and then lay down on my bed. It was my first attempt ever. At first there were small black and red rings before my eyes, but then I went off into sweet slumbers and extraordinary dreams. The next morning I woke up with a sick headache and such a horrible taste in my mouth that I vomited. Tired and listless I fell back again on my bed. Then the door was opened suddenly and Mirella stood in the rectangle of early morning light it let into my room.

She had a newspaper in her hand and there were tears in her eyes. She stared at me. I probably looked at death's door, and I certainly felt like it. Wordlessly she put the newspaper on my bed and left the room. For a while I felt much too weak to raise myself to look at it, but when I finally did so one glance at the banner headline was enough: "Referendum decides for a Republic!" So King Umberto had to go. The monarchy was abolished. The Italian people had declared themselves for a Republic.

I was tired and I felt sicker than ever.

CHAPTER IV

"KISSES YOU DREAM OF"

I occupied a whole apartment in Parioli, five rooms and the usual offices. Parioli is the most modern residential quarter in Rome and it looks a bit like Chicago. In August 1946 the American Office of Strategic Services—known by its initials of course—requisitioned one of its biggest buildings, part of which it used to house the former representatives of the empires of Mussolini and Hitler, temporarily at least.

The place in which I lived—on American sufferance—was provided with a maid, a chauffeur and a library, but none of them was altogether to my liking. The maid was never able to close the windows properly, which meant that the apartment was always draughty. The chauffeur was a former Partisan, which—at that time at least—I did not regard as a recommendation. And the library, in which I would search despairingly for something decent to read, consisted chiefly of works on sex and included, for example, the collected works of Sacher-Masoch on the point. It had been left behind by the former occupant of the flat, a German Countess whose name I never learned. She had lived there mysteriously with her library under Mussolini, and when he went she disappeared equally mysteriously.

My boredom in my luxurious apartment was added to by the bath, a magnificent affair with marble slabs. No matter how hard I tried I could never get a drop of water out of its taps. Neither could the maid, though I doubt if she tried very hard. The chromium plate of the bathroom gleamed elegantly and I sizzled in the hot Roman sun, but there was no water to refresh myself.

When I had read the whole of the library of sexual works—it was no longer a very large one—and sweated in the heat I didn't know what to do with myself. The apartment had everything in the way of domestic appointments, but I was bored to death in it. I felt that the Americans had installed me here only for the sake of my honest face, and perhaps in recollection of my services at the time of the capitulation. It therefore seemed all the more astonishing to me that no one seemed to bother his head about me.

Although, despite my fruitless fiddling with the bath taps, despite the works of Sacher-Masoch, and despite the ill-fitting windows, I much preferred it here to the villa sanatorium with its drug addicts, nevertheless I missed the smell of the blossom and even the cackle of the two old ladies. In my mind I went over the events which had led to my installation here.

One day in my discreet asylum I received a letter. It was in a delicate light-blue envelope and for a moment I thought that some old flame had remembered me. But no sooner had I opened the envelope and taken a glance at the enclosed letter than it immediately became clear that my hopes of any gently sentimental origin were baseless. The following is what I read:

"Dear Eugenio,

With all the secret services in the world searching for you in vain it has fallen to me to discover you tucked away in a mad-house. And as insane Europe can only be built up again by madmen I have taken the liberty of handing on your present address to those who propose to supervise its reconstruction. They will call for you to-morrow. I hope we shall see each other again.

LUIGI PARRILLI."

And that was that. I knew the signatory well of course. He was a Baron, a Knight of the Order of Malta, and a Papal Chamberlain. His father, an admiral, had left him a fortune, but in his youth he had taken steps to incorporate it into the gaming banks of Monte-Carlo. When this process was finally completed and nothing more remained for him to do, except shoot himself, he met the daughter of a rich Italian industrialist, married the girl and rose with that into the highest super-tax brackets. Apart from smoking a hundred cigarettes a day he interested himself passionately in politics, and he did it to such effect that it was solely due to his southern patriotism that General Wolff and

72

I were able to get into touch, via Switzerland, with Allen W. Dulles, the head of the American O.S.S., and finally to sign the capitulation in Caserta.

His relations with the Americans were well known and now that he had found out where I was I resigned myself to being picked up, as he had warned me, by the Americans. And it was just as well that I did because that was exactly what happened. The next day a huge Buick with a U.S. army pennant drew up in front of my private lunatic asylum and under the astonished gaze of the other inmates I was invited to take my seat in it by a huge American Top Sergeant. The Negro chauffeur then drove us off to Rome and on the way we were respectfully greeted by all the carabinieri we came across. On our arrival in Rome I was deposited in this flat and since then I had had little else to do but fiddle with the bath taps in the waning hope that in the end water would appear.

One day when I was reclining in a deck-chair and looking through the books of the Countess for the umpteenth time there was a discreet knock on the door of the room which was supposed to do service as my study. Two types then came in who looked like a music-hall turn: Mutt and Jeff, or the long and short of it. They introduced themselves to me as Jim and Joe of the O.S.S. and shook my hand as though we were long-lost friends.

"We are very glad to have found you, Mr. Dollmann," they assured me.

I had been addressed as Herr, Signor, and even Monsieur. Now it was to be Mr. and I should have to behave myself accordingly. I invited my visitors to sit down and they did so. After which they produced bottles of whisky, packets of chewing gum and large supplies of cigarettes, and began to drink and smoke. I joined in. They inquired solicitously about my "journey", expressed regret that I had been so bothered and assured me that they were very glad to be able to do something for me. So far I had paid more attention to their whisky than to their remarks, but now I grew more attentive. The purpose of their visit was probably about to be revealed.

"And now," said Jim, the long one of the two, "what do you intend to do, Mr. Dollmann?"

"Naturally I'd sooner stay in Italy or somewhere along the Mediterranean if that were possible," I replied, and without giving them an opportunity to make any comment I added: "I should like to devote myself to literature and art once again, and therefore the Mediterranean strikes me as particularly suitable."

At that the short, fat one, Joe, chewed away desperately at his seventh wad of chewing-gum, and the long, thin Jim was obviously embarrassed.

"Well, actually," said Jim, "we had something else in mind for you," and before I could answer he added quickly: "You see, we think you're just the man for the job."

"What job?" I asked cautiously.

Jim quickly swallowed a gulp of whisky.

"Well, you see, for us of the American Secret Service the struggle against Communism is only just beginning," he said.

I took a quick look at the calendar to make quite certain that this really was the year 1946. Jim noticed the direction of my glance.

"Of course, it's top secret, you understand," he said.

"Yes, top secret, of course," repeated little Joe, and folded his hands comfortably over his belly.

I looked at them again and came rapidly to the conclusion that they weren't really suitable instruments in the struggle against one-sixth of the world.

"And so we thought of sending you to Germany on a secret mission," Jim went on. "You would have to take a six-weeks' course, and after that you would be able to build up a really good espionage organization against the Russians. I have already informed my superiors in Washington about what I intend to do with you, and the G.2. General in Caserta has already confirmed the plan. By the way, you'll probably know yourself that even before you came here Baron Parilli discussed the whole matter with General Morgan, our Commander-in-Chief at Caserta, and that they came to a satisfactory agreement about your future."

No, I didn't know that, but it was very consoling to know that it was all so satisfactory.

"But I'd much sooner stay in Italy," I objected. "And if I can't do that I'd like to go to Greece."

The little fellow Joe gave me a dirty look and Jim didn't look any too pleased.

"You can stay here for a while perhaps," he said slowly, "but in view of the nature of the struggle we aren't particularly interested in the Mediterranean. Our new frontier lies in Germany. . . ."

He was talking like a young university lecturer who dabbled a bit in espionage in his spare time.

"But with my name and my past reputation I can hardly . . ." I began, but little Joe interrupted me:

"We're the masters of the world now," he exclaimed. "No one can touch you."

Whilst I looked at his rather bibulous little eyes and his distended belly his colleague hastily smoothed over his gaffe.

"So you don't want to? Very well, but think it over. You can stay here for a while. Do you need money?"

I nodded and he pushed a bundle of notes towards me over the table.

"By the way, you needn't frequent just those places where everyone knows you," he said. "And here's a little document you'll find useful. It says you're the employee of an American organization—false name, of course—and you can safely go anywhere you like with it."

"But I'm not an employee of any American organization."

Both of them dismissed the objection as ridiculous.

"Doesn't matter," they said in unison. "Doesn't matter at all."

They got up and shook hands with me. Nothing further was said about anti-Russian espionage.

"Well, good-bye, Mr. Dollmann. And if you need anything. . . . Well, you know where to find us."

'I certainly do,' I thought as I looked out of the window at the jeep with American military police that drove slowly past the house. In the meantime, talking loudly to each other, the two blundered out. Down below in the street I saw them taking a note of the house number and obviously comparing it with the one in their note-books to make quite sure that I really lived there. The jeep drew up and they both got in and were driven off.

Now if I had put the false identity card away in my wallet and continued my reading of Sacher-Masoch's memoirs I should never have ended up in the hands of the Roman police. But unfortunately I was seized by a fit of daring and a desire to try out the efficacy of my new papers so I got up and left the the house, discarding all my previous precautions such as dark glasses and a false beard, and walking light-heartedly through the streets of the city that significantly carried a she-wolf in her coat of arms.

That was bad enough, but worse was the wicked angel that suggested that I should go to Trastevere. Now Trastevere is notoriously red and most of its inhabitants were Communists or their sympathisers and therefore not likely to be well disposed towards me. However, I made my way to the house in Trastevere in which my former chauffeur now lived together with my former maid, whom he had married; the pair of them having in the meantime produced a numerous Roman family.

Luigi, which was my former chauffeur's name, and Rosina, my former maid, greeted me with loud acclamation—there were even tears from Rosina. She also lost no time in putting a dish of spaghetti before me which could reasonably have lasted me a week, whilst Luigi kept filling up my glass with golden Frascati wine. Whilst eating and drinking I inquired how things had gone with them.

"Oh," replied Luigi with a trace of embarrassment but with some satisfaction, "things have gone very well really. Shortly after you went the Americans arrived. . . ."

"Ah!" I murmured. I had already noticed that on my own. There were Jim and Joe for example.

"And Rome got an American Town Commandant," Luigi went on. "And very soon he sent for me. The military police came for me, Colonel. I thought I was going to be shot. They can't get the Colonel, I thought, so they're going to get his chauffeur. But when I got there the American Commandant said: 'Luigi Rossi, you were the chauffeur of the German Colonel Dollmann and so you must know all the places where he used to go.'"

At this point Luigi scratched himself behind the ear and looked more embarrassed than ever. I had nearly finished my spaghetti and that and the Frascati wine had put me into a very charitable and tolerant mood. In any case, it would have been silly to be in any other mood, for Luigi could have called in the local Partisans at any moment. I was also interested to discover why Luigi hadn't been shot after all.

"Carry on, Luigi," I said encouragingly. "I quite understand your awkward position."

Whereupon Luigi proceeded without further embarrassment.

"Then he told me to show him all the places where you used to drink in the evening, and so on, and so I did. And then he said I could have fifty litres of petrol a week as a reward . . ."

"And what else do you think the American said?" burst in Rosina indignantly. "He said that if Luigi took more than fifty litres he'd be shot. My Luigi!"

Luigi was feeling very proud of himself now, secure in the admiration and sympathy of his wife and certain of my understanding tolerance. I must say that I was really very glad that nothing had happened to Luigi and that he now even enjoyed high American connections and the right to fifty litres of petrol a week.

After a while, when we had discussed this and that, and recalled various interesting things—and drunk a good deal of the Frascati wine—Luigi suggested that we should go out and celebrate our reunion in a *trattoria,* the sort where amongst rather primitive and vulgar pictures of Bacchus there is always a statue of the Blessed Virgin Mary in the place of honour. Naturally I demurred. It would be lunacy, I thought, to go into such a place in this red quarter of the town, but despite my more and more vigorous objections Luigi, who was well lit up by this time, wouldn't take no for an answer and despite my protests he went off gaily in search of his friends, leaving me still discussing with Rosina the impossibility of the proposed celebration.

"But listen, Rosina, I can't possibly go into a *trattoria* in this part of the world."

"Why not, Colonel? After all, everyone likes you here; you were so good to us all when you were here."

But whilst I was still shaking my head obstinately the sound of singing was heard as Luigi returned with his friends.

"Think of all the people you saved from being shot," Rosina urged. "And from the raids. And then you started up the Black Market where we could buy all the things we wanted and couldn't get otherwise. And then . . ."

I think she would have gone on enumerating all my good deeds, but at that moment Luigi burst in with his friends.

"They're all Communists!" I exclaimed in horror.

Rosina looked at me without understanding.

"Of course they are," she said, "but what does that matter?"

At that time I hadn't made the acquaintance of Don Camillo's Peppone and I thought it mattered a lot, and I also thought that whereas they had probably forgotten their rescue from shooting and the benefits of the Black Market, these new masters of the poorer quarters of Rome had not altogether forgotten the German Colonel Dollmann. However, a few hours later when I was sitting amongst them listening to the strains of the "Marseillaise" I thought they were all the best fellows in the world. The Americans had ungratefully forgotten my services in connection with the capitulation, but all these Communists had a lively remembrance of past benefits and they now plied me with wine and presents, singing at the tops of their voices. Luigi had raised half the local population which, armed to the teeth, then enthusiastically accompanied me to the *trattoria* and cheered me to the echo.

Their automatic pistols lay on the table in front of me and two strong men with bushy eyebrows sat on each side of me, arm in arm with me and swaying happily from left to right as they sang. All the poor people of Rome seemed to be gathered round to do me honour and see that nothing happened to me. In the warm, smoky atmosphere of the low-ceilinged *trattoria*, amidst the tinkling of guitars and zithers, and the singing of all the folksongs imaginable, the women stood around, young and old, fat and slim, some with babies sucking at their breasts, whilst their menfolk drank my health in glass after glass.

The affair ended in the general singing of "Santa Lucia". The Communists clattered their weapons like the ancient Romans and the young women began to dance with their boy friends. I declared that now I must go at last, whereupon a strong escort of armed men formed up to accompany me and we all marched out to the strains of the "Marseillaise", the men singing lustily and staggering a bit, but all obviously happy at being able to show their gratitude to "their Colonel" for the services he had once been able to render them. If I had told them where I was now living at the behest of the O.S.S. I think they would certainly have provided me with a bodyguard, but before we reached the street in which my apartment was situated I thought it wiser to part company with them, and this was then done amidst mutual compliments and great friendliness all round.

I hadn't as yet tested my new identity papers, but at least I was now sure of the good will of the Communists of Rome, which so heartened and encouraged me that I began to grow more and more confident. I extended my trips around Rome, occasionally passing through the Communist quarters in order to have it confirmed by the friendly greeting of the former Partisans, still armed to the teeth, that my popularity amongst them was no passing phase. Actually my feeling of confidence and security was quite misplaced, as I was soon to discover.

During one of my strolls through the centre of Rome— already I dared to show my face on the great square of St. Peter's and in the Vatican Museum—I passed the Villa Parrhasio of Donna Virginia Agnelli. Abandoned and a little dilapidated the ochre-coloured palace of the Fiat heritage lay in the poor quarter of Rome. Dirty children and slatternly women filled the streets around it. Donna Virginia Agnelli, by birth Princess Bourbon del Monte, by marriage widow of Agnelli, the owner of the Fiat works, who crashed in a sports plane whilst flying over Rome, and by inclination (presumably) mistress of an Italian author, who was the centre of more scandals than any of his kind, had a great reputation in these parts. The poor of the neighbourhood worshipped her as the Lady Bountiful of their world and Donna Virginia was too clever not to accept and consolidate her position in their eyes.

The parties she gave in her house surrounded by the tropical scent of wisteria were famous for their magnificence and the poor people of Travestere accepted her house as an oasis of riches in the desert of their poverty and perhaps as something like the fulfilment of their own secret dreams. Donna Virginia was not a beautiful woman, but she was a very attractive and highly desirable one. And she had something beyond her Gobelin decorated palace, her ailing children, her fleet of Fiat limousines and her vast wealth, and that was, surprisingly, a burning patriotism, and she served her country with extraordinary energy and determination. It was she who in 1944 put General Wolff and me in direct touch with the Pope, a connection which ultimately led to the opening of the capitulation negotiations.

And it was at this time that she demonstrated her practical relationship to the real people of Rome. In May, a few days before the capitulation, when you could already hear the sound of artillery fire from Nettuno, she was about to leave Rome, her Vatican mission having been accomplished. But before leaving she stood up in her great car in front of her palace, wearing gold high-laced Roman sandals, a white dress, a gold Spanish belt and a blouse of Venetian lace, and distributed largesse to a cheering crowd surrounding the car, throwing presents to "her" people, the Communists to be of Trastevere. The clothes and toys of her son Gianni, her own brocade evening dresses, innumerable pairs of boots and shoes, many bottles of perfume and pots of cosmetics were thrown to the mob, and all around her the men and women cheered, laughed, and shouted "*Evviva Donna Virginia!*" And when the distribution was over they escorted her car enthusiastically to the road that was to lead her to safety.

They never saw her again. That road led not to safety but to death. She died in a car accident. And now her palace lay there in the burning sun, surrounded by flowers, but abandoned, its shutters closed across the windows, and the only sign of life was a lame porter who limped across the park.

Leaving this quarter of the poor I wandered into the business streets of the town, still not bothering in the least about my personal safety, for not only were the Americans friendly towards me but the Communists were on my side, and in this way I happened to come to the shop of Signor Giorgio Bulgari. In the elegant window of the most fashionable jeweller in Rome lay a number of valuable stones and pieces of jewellery. I looked at them idly and then I had the impression that I had seen them somewhere before. I racked my brains—since my period in camp my memory no longer seemed so accurate. And just when I was about to give it up with shaking head and go on my way in continued boredom, it all came back to me. Yes, I certainly did know those stones.

I made the acquaintance of the brothers Bulgari in the winter of 1943–4, having been invited to their house through some distant acquaintance of mine. Giorgio Bulgari was a big and corpulent Levantine who was already losing his hair. His brother was very different, small and lean and more like a scholar. It was he who led me through innumerable corridors and out under the river Tiber where their strong rooms were situated. As we went under the river the walls and ceilings were damp, and now and again drops of water fell onto my smart uniform. There was a red room for rubies, a blue room for sapphires and a green room for emeralds. The place was like the underground dungeons of the Borgias, except that it was lighted by neon tubes and everything was mechanised. The pressure of a finger on a button was sufficient to cause the walls to open out and reveal precious stones displayed on marble slabs.

Whilst I sat there and marvelled, and drank one glass of Napoleon brandy after the other, Giorgio's brother—no doubt in order to impress me—conjured what he described as the Crown Jewels of the late Tsar out of those same rock walls. They had, he said, been entrusted to the Bulgaris by the Soviet Government for sale to the United States, and here they were, lying under the Tiber. The crown of diamonds worn by the late Tsarina was there and I was allowed to hold it in my hands for closer inspection. And all those jewels that had once graced the court of the Tsar were now in the keeping of two Levantines for sale to the highest bidder.

At last Bulgari returned all the jewels to their place of safety, poured me out a final glass of brandy and came to the point. I had known already that there would be one. I was, somehow or other, to transfer a bar of gold to Greece on his account for the benefit of his despairing relatives there. On consideration I decided that to secure the good offices of such influential people as these two brothers was worth a little trouble so in the end I agreed. I took charge of the gold bar and sent Lieutenant Gärtner of the German General Staff in Italy off to Athens with it in an army car and hoped for the best.

For weeks I heard nothing from him and after a while I felt quite certain that the German military police had caught him with the forbidden gold and that it was now only a matter of time before I too would be arrested as the instigator of the illegal transaction. However, Gärtner had arrived quite safely and delivered up the gold to the Bulgari clan in Athens. In return they had dined him and wined him in the utmost luxury for four weeks on part at least of the proceeds from the disposal of the gold. As I was told subsequently, Gärtner wasn't sober for weeks and it is a matter for some astonishment that he managed to keep his mouth shut.

In the meantime the Bulgaris in Rome continued to do business with the occupying authorities and I lived on tenterhooks. When Gärtner finally returned safely to Rome about a month later, having finally succeeded in dragging himself away from the hospitable Bulgaris in Athens, the German forces were preparing to evacuate Rome and the Bulgaris there were preparing to do business with the next lot of occupiers.

All this went swiftly through my mind whilst I stood in front of the window and I decided to find out whether my old friend Giorgio was as fat as ever, so I opened the door and walked into the shop. A little assistant came up and bowed to me. On account of my shabby British rain-coat he no doubt decided that I was a high American officer in civilian clothes. No one but a high-up would venture into his shop in such a state.

"What can I do for you, sir," he inquired politely.

"I want to see Signor Giorgio," I said.

At that the little assistant must have been quite certain that his original assumption was correct, for he hurried off to the rear and after a moment or two Giorgio himself appeared through the door with his features properly composed for the sale of expensive jewellery. He was, in fact, as fat as ever—even fatter perhaps—but, above all, the look of disappointment that caused his jowls to fall when he saw me was comic. However, he switched on a smile again and came forward to greet me.

He treated me just as he would have treated any other prospective client, led me once again into the subterranean vaults and once again offered me a brandy. But his hands shook and I realized that he was horrified at the thought that someone might discover me on his premises. Finally he could stand the suspense no longer.

"But, Herr Dollmann, aren't you afraid of the Americans?"

"Not in the least," I said, and inwardly I was enjoying his terror. "Why should I be? I am here under their special protection."

His astonishment at this piece of information was enormous. He could hardly have been more surprised if I had attempted to steal one of his jewels under his very nose. Then he opened his fleshy lips, and whilst I was wondering just what he would say if I showed him my American papers, he said: "Oh! under American protection!"

It seemed to reassure him and once again the rather greasy smile appeared round his lips and he poured me out another brandy. And with all the facile charm he used to camouflage his business intentions he observed:

"You know, we were all afraid that you had been killed."

' "Afraid" is good,' I thought, but out loud I declared with more confidence than I felt: "How very amusing! People like me don't just disappear for ever like that."

And then suddenly Giorgio and the whole business sickened me and I decided to get out. He accompanied me to the door politely, bowed very formally and, with a face that contradicted his words, expressed the hope that I would honour the place with my presence again.

I never did. That was the last time I was in the Bulgari vaults under the Tiber.

After this foray I felt the need for a little fresh air and I went into the Wolkonsky Park. The Villa Wolkonsky had been presented to Princess Wolkonsky by Tsar Alexander I as a reward for certain discreet but far from ambiguous services to his royal person and at a later date it had become the German Embassy in Rome. It was now requisitioned by the British. An old porter let me into the park and as I stood once again under the old Roman aqueduct and looked at the rose garden, which had been allowed to grow a little wild in the meantime, I remembered that it was from this very garden that the *Gestapo* had taken Princess Mafalda of Savoy away to the terrible fate that awaited her in Dachau.

Slowly I walked through the park again towards the villa itself. At the bottom of the broad steps a large car was waiting, flying the pennant of the British Commandant. I sat down idly on an old mossy bank surrounded by the romantic smell of roses in full bloom and as I looked at the British pennant it seemed to grow redder and I recalled the odd incident with the Russian Ambassador that had taken place in that very house when it was the German Embassy.

It was in 1940 and the German Ambassador was Herr von Mackensen. He was to be the last for some time. His wife rang me up and asked me to present myself in gala uniform as they were expecting the visit of the Russian Ambassador, a woman. The gala uniform was no doubt to do her the honours in style. I arrived there neat and clean as a new pin with my cords and tassels dangling impressively from my shoulders, and after a while a big black car drove up. Importantly I went forward to greet the Ambassador, and a small rather shrivelled woman got out of the car, but she was dressed in a wonderful cloak of white ermine which reached down to the ground. Obviously ill at ease and constantly looking round at her escort she came forward towards us. I gave her one of my best bows and greeted her with the word "Excellency", which seemed to please her no end. Smiling a little nervously she allowed herself to be ushered into the vestibule of the Wolkonsky Palace, where the waiting footmen came forward to relieve her of her astonishing ermine cloak, but she wasn't having any. She held it tightly over her rather shrunken bosom and said *"Nyet! Nyet! Nyet!"* It was a word Allied diplomats were subsequently to hear very often from their Russian colleagues. When the footmen failed and perforce retired, I tried my luck, but with no greater success. The representative of the Red Tsar wasn't letting that ermine cloak out of her sight.

It was a very hot day, but she even sat down to tea in it, and as sweat was visibly pouring down her face, one of us would again suggest from time to time that she should discard the oppressive garment, only to be met again with a determined *"Nyet, nyet, nyet!"* Her behaviour was a complete mystery and finally Frau von Mackensen asked her pleasantly why she was unwilling to discard it—it was so very hot; she would be more comfortable without it. The Russian representative first looked under the table as though she wanted to make quite certain that there was no microphone there to record her words, and then she said shyly:

"I can't let it out of my sight. It was sent me specially from Moscow for this reception."

So we were to be impressed sartorially too. Frau von Mackensen betrayed a sudden interest in the ceiling and I hardly knew where to look. In the meantime our guest continued to sit there in her wonderful ermine cloak and drink tea and sweat. When we were able to give her our attention again she explained that it was the coronation cloak of the dowager Tsarina and that she had been told that she must treat it with the utmost care. She also told us that she was the daughter of a factory worker, and as she sat there with a shining nose and the sweat running down her face the revelation seemed less surprising: she looked as though she had just stopped work at the bench herself to drink a cup of tea. Soon after that she left and, still wrapped up in the precious ermine cloak of the dowager Tsarina of Russia, she tottered back to her car.

I had occasion to ride in that car later on. In its roof there were a number of nozzles, and various perfumes could be sprayed down into the car as the requisite buttons on a panel were pressed.

In the meantime the British Commandant's car had driven off and I got up and left the park too, left it to its overpowering smell of roses and my memories of the Russian Ambassador and her ermine cloak. As I passed one of the many statues in the park the thought occurred to me of going out to Cerveteri and seeing the Etruscan graves there again. I had nothing to do with my time and Cerveteri, or Caere, had always interested me. It was an ancient trading centre. Surrounded by pine trees and the rolling hills of the Campagna were not only the Etruscan graves that have made the place famous but also the palace of the ancient Ruspoli family. Prince Francesco Ruspoli was an old friend of mine and it occurred to me that perhaps he might be in a position to help me. In addition, the old graves attracted me more than did the suspicious looks—or so I thought them— of the Roman carabinieri. In my pocket I had the false identity card the Americans had given me, so nothing much could happen to me, and, in any case, less was likely to happen amongst the ancient graves than here in Rome. Money I had too, quite enough to pay for a return ticket to Cerveteri. The next morning therefore I went to the railway station, bought my ticket—cheapest class—and went off in the direction of Pisa.

At Palo I got out and there I took a country bus, an old bone-shaker that seemed to be made entirely of bits of junked American army cars. But it got me safely to Cerveteri. Two hours after leaving my flat I was walking through the ancient graves of the Etruscans. Those old graves hewn out of the solid rock have always had a strange fascination for me. Those who first found them, robbed them of everything of value, but not of their gloomy mysterious atmosphere. In their dark grottoes —the oldest of them dates from the seventh century B.C.—I never felt myself depressed and burdened by thoughts of death. There was one in particular that exercised a great attraction on me. It was perhaps half a mile from the others, out of the way and deserted. Visitors were even less likely there. The sun was shining down warmly and I was looking forward to the coolness of the grotto behind its screen of dwarf cypresses. I went into the grotto and around me were black and red Etrus-can vases. I had not been there long, however, when behind me I heard a sound. I got up from where I had been sitting and to my astonishment and misgiving I saw someone at the entrance to the grotto. I went up cautiously and in the gloom I saw it was a slim young woman in a long dark riding habit wearing a three-cornered hat over her blonde curls. A few seconds later and those blonde curls were against my cheek, my lips were on her lips and our joyful tears mingled with each other. It was really very romantic.

The lady in the riding habit was Bibi, a girl I had met ten years before in her mother's little boarding house in Rome. Her real name was Marie-Celeste but everyone called her Bibi and so did I. She was almost as tall as me and very slim, almost too delicately built, but that didn't stop my falling in love with her, and she had a really lovely face. I had taken her out of her mother's boarding house and introduced her to Roman society, into which she fitted admirably. I don't know why, but I suddenly remembered that she was a very delicate eater, chicken livers and things like that, and I laughed. She dropped her arms and struck me with the riding whip she was carrying.

"What are you laughing about, Eugenio?" she asked sharply, but her own face was radiant.

"I think it's the oddest thing to meet you in an Etruscan grave after so many years," I said.

She turned, and as I followed her to the door I wondered where she had got her expensive riding habit from.

"A good many things have changed in those years," she said.

I agreed with her and immediately asked her about the riding habit.

"You'll see when you come outside."

I had no intention of staying behind in the grave, but when I did go outside into the sunshine again and had stopped blinking I was astonished at the two magnificent Arabian stallions and the liveried groom who was holding them and apparently waiting for Bibi. On the man's hat was the coat of arms of the Ruspoli family. Bibi looked first at the horses and then at me.

"Well?" she said.

I suppose my face must have been a picture, for she began to laugh.

"That surprises you, doesn't it?"

It certainly did.

"What's happened, Bibi?" I asked. "Have you become a lady companion in the house of the Ruspolis?"

"In a kind of way," she said, and she beckoned to the groom who led the two horses forward and bowed respectfully.

"Mount," she said. "I'll explain everything on the way."

I looked at the well-groomed horse before me, the beautiful leather saddle with the Ruspoli arms in brass on it, and the noble eyes of the beast as it looked at me and then I glanced down at my worn and baggy trousers.

"I can't ride like this," I said.

With the aid of the groom Bibi had already mounted and sat side-saddle looking down at me imperiously.

"It's really quite a gentle horse," she said. "He won't do you any harm."

That observation stung me so much that without more ado I swung myself into the saddle. But on the way back she tantalisingly refused to say a word about herself and insisted on hearing my whole story from beginning to end. By the time I had finished we were at the Ruspoli palace. It was a mediaeval building with high, thick crenellated walls, dungeons, towers, and so many rooms that no one knew exactly how many. It might have been a stronghold of the Borgias, but for the moment it looked as though it all belonged to Bibi, for as we went into the place all the servants we met bowed to her respectfully. We made our way into a Renaissance hall in which the Ruspolis of old had held carousals and I felt more than ever out of place in my baggy trousers. Bibi flung off her hat, tossed aside her riding crop and dropped into a comfortable arm-chair as though she were at home, and at that moment a soft-footed servant appeared carrying a tray with Campari, soda, ice and glasses. By this time my curiosity was at fever pitch.

"Tell me, Bibi, what's the idea? You're behaving here as though the place belonged to you."

"It does," she replied, enjoying my astonishment. "All of it."

Astonishment is really not quite the word to describe my feelings. I felt almost as though someone had suddenly pulled the chair from under me.

"What's happened to Ruspoli?" I demanded.

"Nothing," she said. "Except that I married him. And when I come to think of it," she added thoughtfully, "you were responsible for that."

"Me!" I almost shrieked. "How?"

"Well, he knew you before he knew me, but we first met in an internment camp."

"How did you get there?"

"Because we were both your friends. The bond of union, you see."

It wasn't the first time that I had the feeling that this was an unjust world. Whilst camp for me had meant endless bother with Allied military police and Intelligence Officers, for her it had meant the first step to becoming one of the greatest ladies in Italy.

She was now nibbling at a dish of chicken liver that had been placed before her, and as I sipped my Campari I looked at her and it seemed to me that no time at all had passed since I first met her, sitting in her mother's drawing-room and eating chicken liver and salbri—a little more girlish perhaps then, a little less mature, but after all she had been only sixteen. I lived in her mother's boarding house at the time because it was a cheerful, lively sort of place where you met a good many people, and, naturally, a good many young women too. There was drinking and dancing, and very often the evening at the Pension Rossi, as it was called, didn't end until the morning sun was beginning to show over the hills of the Eternal City. In those days Bibi was madly in love with a man who had started off in life as a street arab in Trastevere but who had worked himself up and was then a rich timber merchant. Bibi was waiting patiently for him to marry her, which he would probably have done but for the fact that a motoring accident put a sudden end to his life.

For quite a while after that Bibi was not to be seen and when she finally re-appeared she looked more beautiful than ever and I was much drawn to her. It took me quite a while to penetrate her almost Anglo-Saxon reserve, but in the end I succeeded and she became my girl friend. Obviously, such a relationship was practically impossible to conceal, and I had no particular interest in concealing it, so I began to take her out to balls and other functions at the Embassy and in Roman society generally. She fitted in wonderfully and she became very popular indeed, so much so that I gradually became less and less important. After a while I sent her to relatives of mine in Germany, and there, in Tegernsee and in Vienna, she became equally popular and equally sought after. After she had succeeded in freeing old Count Cini from Dachau she returned to Italy.

Count Cini had been one of Mussolini's ministers but the Germans gradually came to distrust him and in the end they suspected him of funny business and put him away in Dachau. He was already an old man then and his son came to me in the hope that Wolff and I could do something for his father. Once again I used my so often exploited connections and as the young Italian spoke no German I gave him Bibi as a companion and

sent him off on the mission. Bibi proved a better key to concentration camp doors than any letters of mine and the old man
was freed. In this way Bibi, the saving angel, became a very
welcome guest in one of the richest houses in Italy. In general
she had a wonderful knack of making all highly-placed and
influential people like her.

The Reichsführer of the S.S. was in Rome and wanted to go
out incognito, for which purpose he borrowed one of my suits,
which, incidentally, didn't fit him very well. I knew that he
wanted to buy Christmas presents and I had no desire to waste
my time with him so I made an arrangement with Bibi to meet
us in the most expensive establishment in town, then I put
Himmler into a car and drove straight there. When we walked
into the shop she was already there as arranged and she came
up to us and greeted me as an old friend she was meeting quite
accidentally. Himmler took the bait. He kept whispering into
my ear how attractive he found her, which amused me because
she was not at all the S.S. type of beauty he ought to have been
struck with. I took no notice of him, but he kept on whispering
and digging me in the ribs with his elbow, looking eagerly at
the tall and elegant Bibi through his lop-sided pince-nez.

When I had kept him dangling long enough I consented to
introduce him—later on as an afterthought he was to reproach
me with my decadent taste: only a fellow like me would consent
to associate with such an un-Germanic type. But at the time
he was tremendously smitten with Bibi and he was delighted
when—hearing of his mission—she offered to assist him in
making his purchases. You could see him being more and
more unfaithful in his mind to the Scholtz-Klinck type of
German beauty. The business took us an hour and when we
drove off the car smelt like a lady's boudoir with all his
purchases. Still strongly under the influence of Bibi's "really
rather decadent" attractions Himmler proposed that we should
drive out to the coast and have lunch somewhere there and this
we did before we returned to Rome. On our arrival I got rid
of Himmler and ever after that Bibi was above all suspicion for
the chief of the German S.S. The acquaintance stood her in
good stead later on. With the astonishing instinct of the female
she started to learn English and this aroused the suspicion of

Kappler, the head of the Security Service in Rome, and shortly before we evacuated the Eternal City she would certainly have been arrested if Kappler had dared to lay hands on Himmler's protégée. The result was that until the end she was able to continue dining with me. Another guest was Prince Francesco Ruspoli, and Bibi took such a fancy to him that when we finally had to go she refused to go with me northwards but remained behind in Rome with Ruspoli.

When the Allies arrived the two of them were arrested as having been friends of mine and they were interned together. During their internment their friendship strengthened into love and Francesco promised to marry her as soon as they were free. I knew what had happened to them and during my interrogations I intervened on their behalf with Major Bridge, asking him to take steps with the proper authorities to secure their release, and this he consented to do. A few months later my ex-girl-friend Bibi and my friend Francesco Ruspoli, Prince of the Holy Roman Empire, were married. I could see what she meant when she said that in a way I had been responsible for it.

"So that's how it was!" I exclaimed, and I took a gulp of wine.

"That's how it was," she said and she laughed. "I'm going to change now. Afterwards we'll drive into Rome together."

It took her an hour to change, but at last she was ready and we got into the elegant Lancia which was waiting for us at the gates with the arms of the Ruspoli on its doors and were driven off to Rome. There we sat behind the uniformed chauffeur, Bibi in a model afternoon gown and me in my very dilapidated and unpressed suit.

At the Ruspoli Palace in Rome we found Bibi's step-son Dario, a child of Ruspoli's first marriage. He was wearing a soft silk shirt open at the neck, a wide pair of grey flannel bags, a pair of ringed socks which were not held up by suspenders, and a pair of suede-leather shoes. Only the signet ring of the Brazilian coffee king Materazzo indicated the source of wealth which paid for his life of extravagance. Piled up by generations of Brazilian coffee barons, his mother had brought it with her into the Ruspoli family. Dario had grown up in luxury. He had never known what it was to want and not have and he was already as well known in the night clubs of London and Paris as he was in Rome.

"Come in," he said, and his slim, small-boned hand made an elegant gesture towards the great entrance hall of the palace.

The portraits of his ancestors, men and women with broad, clear-cut faces, some of them hard and brutal, lined the gloomy walls in great dusty gold frames. Under heavy balconies and surrounded by walls many feet thick stood Dario Ruspoli, the descendant of men who had worn the Roman toga, the representative of the new type of European high society.

And with him was Bibi, my former girl friend, a little lady of the lower middle class who had been flushed to the surface of Europe's aristocracy by a series of unlikely events. She was delicate too, too pale, altogether too fine, and much too slim. She was in an elegant afternoon dress now, the young step-mother of Dario and one of the richest women in Italy. With a long silver cigarette holder in her hand she looked up at her husband's ancestors. The cold eyes of the men and women in the great oil paintings looked down without charity at the little nobody who bore their name and was now a princess of the decadent Roman Empire.

The expensive platinum wrist-watch Dario was wearing flashed for a moment in the sun that fell through the old stained-glass windows into the hall. I stood there with them in my shabby suit and all the Ruspolis on the walls seemed no more to approve of me than they did of Bibi. I had a bad conscience and I felt out of place. My suit was old and worn and my face bore the traces of recent privations; I had no watch, no rings and no valuables. There I stood, rather dusty and care-worn, under the critical eyes of the Roman rulers of other days, and it was only by the grace of Jim and Joe the two gum-chewing officers of the O.S.S. that I was there at all. Without their false papers I should have been in a far less pleasant place. The Roman nobles looked down on me superciliously. But their world was dead and gone whilst mine was still there—thanks to the secret police of the New World.

Altogether the three of us were a wonderful cross-cut of modern European civilization. Bibi and Dario dropped their cigarettes onto the stone flags of the palace hall and put their well-shod feet on them. After that we had tea. Bibi talked about her horses, Dario talked about various parties and his latest conquests, and I talked about my escape. Our conversation was interrupted by a call from the American Embassy for Bibi, and by Dario's remembering that he had an appointment with a lady who belonged to his reserve of conquests.

"Eugenio," said Bibi, "I've got to go to a cocktail party at the American Embassy. Will you wait here for me?"

I didn't care much for the idea of being left alone in this old palace with the disapproving ancestors so I tried to keep her.

"Don't tell me you'll be seeing our old friend Mr. B——!" I said.

"Mr. B——?" she queried. "Who's he? I can't remember him."

"Why, the American Embassy man who used to give those fantastic parties in that castle on the coast."

At that she remembered, came away from the door and began to laugh.

"Yes, of course, I remember now. Mario, Mario, let's have some more Martinis."

She sat down again, ready to talk about our American friend, and I sat down too, much relieved that I had been able to prevent her from going.

Mario brought the Martinis and we sat there sipping them.

"That was the fellow who used to bring lorry loads of boys from Trastevere for his parties, wasn't it?" Bibi said.

"That's right. Mr. B——, of the United States Embassy," and I began to laugh at the memory.

Mr. B—— was a rich industrialist from the middle West. In return for I don't know what services to his country the United States Government had sent him to Italy. He had a salary, I suppose, but it was quite clear that he must have drawn liberally on his private means to live the sort of life he lived when he got there.. At first he was a very important person, a representative of the American Government. He was, however, more concerned with parties than with diplomatic activity. Many members of the Roman aristocracy and of the Diplomatic

Corps were invited to these parties, but nevertheless they can hardly be said to have been held primarily in the representative interests of the United States, for Mr. B—— was very interested in the well-built youth of the working-class quarter of Trastevere. Later on however these same youths were to render the United States Government other services as Partisans. In the meantime Mr. B—— needed them for little affairs which were not to be regulated with hand grenades or automatics.

"Do you remember the climax of it all?" I asked, after our fourth Martini.

"I certainly do," she replied.

It was the evening when the arrival of a new Ambassador was expected. It actually ended Mr. B——'s official activity altogether. The new Ambassador was hardly the type to be welcomed with one of Mr. B——'s parties. However, he had organized this party and invited members of the Diplomatic Corps and of the Roman aristocratic élite as usual, and the party took place, again as usual, in the castle by the sea.

That evening a few hours before the festivities were due to begin, a lorry was sent to Trastevere, where, in return for a financial consideration, he hired a band of tough and muscular young Romans and brought them to the coast. The official part of the programme for them was to form a guard of honour down the steps in front of the palace, wearing the dress of Medici pages and carrying lighted torches, to receive the guests. Their costumes were cut very tightly and showed off their nobler parts; as each new guest arrived they all had to bow low, which involved a great danger of splitting their pants, something which did, of course, occasionally happen.

Something else which happened, but quite regularly, was that when certain intimate friends of Mr. B—— from the Roman aristocracy arrived and disappeared in to the upper rooms of the castle, the ranks of the waiting Medici link-boys would be diminished to that extent.

"Do you remember the Ambassador's face when he arrived, Bibi?" I inquired.

It had certainly been a picture. The party was in full swing and the number of Medici pages still waiting on the stone steps for late guests was already greatly reduced when a big American car flying the pennant of the United States Embassy drove up. Out of it descended the new American Ambassador to the Court of Rome, and his family, which consisted of his wife and his two daughters.

When Mr. B—— came down the steps to greet his guest the first sight that met his eyes was one of the daughters being carried back into the car. The other, apparently being made of sterner stuff, was still on her feet. The tight pants of one of the pages had burst, causing the contretempts. Mr. B—— smiled. The Ambassador did not smile. They stood there in the flickering light of the torches and looked at each other: the fast-living business tycoon and the Quaker Ambassador. The latter was tall and thin, like all the other members of his family, and he wore large horn-rimmed glasses through which his pale blue eyes stared at Mr. B——. His eyes were screwed up as though he were short sighted, and perhaps because he could hardly believe the evidence they placed before him. His wife wore a summer dress as creased as her face, and she too had large horn-rimmed glasses. On her upper lip was more than the trace of a dark moustache. The one daughter still visible was very much like her, except that her moustache was blonde. When his wife had finished her indignant flow, the Ambassador told Mr. B—— in a few well-chosen words just what he thought of him and his goings on, then he turned abruptly on his heel, handed his wife and remaining daughter back into the car, got in himself and was driven off, leaving Mr. B—— standing there looking after the car, still smiling. After all, he had his business in America to go back to. And go back to it he did—within three days.

That evening I was back in my flat, bored to death and extracting what amusement I could from the life's work of the Marquis de Sade, when I remembered the business with Frau Scholtz-Klinck, the Nazi Women's leader, lauded as the perfect type of German womanhood. It was in 1938. I received her at the station and accompanied her to the headquarters of the Fascist Party to meet its chief, Achilles Starace. Incidentally, his Christian name had not been given him for nothing and the ladies of Roman high society surrounded him with their attentions. He was a very handsome, powerful man and he wore at least three different uniforms every day. Every morning, for example, he would go riding in the Borghese Park in a white uniform.

When I arrived with Frau Scholtz-Klinck she was obviously deeply impressed with so much manly beauty and elegance and it was my job to translate for her benefit the extremely flowery speech with which he greeted her. At first everything went off without embarrassment and Frau Scholtz-Klinck, "the First Lady of the Reich" as Starace called her, looked around delightedly at all the handsome young uniformed Fascists who had been mobilised to meet her. Then Starace apparently thought that the time had come for a little suggestion he had in mind, particularly as "the First Lady of the Reich" was obviously very keen and went out of her way to express her regret that she would be staying such a short time.

"But, dearest comrade," said Starace sweetly, "we shall be seeing you in Campo Dux."

Scholtz-Klinck turned to me:

"Campo Dux, what's that?"

"It's the big sport camp of the Fascist Youth," I explained, and her face lit up; she was keen on men.

"You will be surrounded only by young men, dearest comrade," Starace put in. "Eighty thousand sturdy, handsome young Fascists."

"Eighty thousand!" exclaimed Scholtz-Klinck. Eighty thousand young and handsome ones!

Seeing her enthusiasm Starace now let himself go:

"You will be the Goddess of our camp, dearest comrade!" he exclaimed lyrically. "You will be surrounded by eighty thousand worshippers. But only one will be your knight."

Frau Scholtz-Klinck's eyes were shining now.

"Oh!" she exclaimed. "Who?"

Starace crossed his arms over his breast and stood before her in a strong-man pose.

"I," he said simply.

"How charming!" returned Scholtz-Klinck, obviously thrilled at the thought.

By this time I was beginning to feel uncomfortable. It began to look to me as though Achilles Starace was promising himself a little bit of fun with the "First Lady of the Reich". I didn't want to be a spoil-sport, but after all, she was an official representative and I felt I had some responsibility in the matter. There was already a certain amount of suppressed amusement amongst the German officers who were there with the German Ambassador von Mackensen.

"And I alone will stand before your tent, dearest comrade," went on Starace, and his voice grew tender.

'Like hell you will,' I thought, but out loud I said:

"Perhaps you would allow me to offer an observation on the subject?"

Starace glared at me and Frau Scholtz-Klinck looked eager.

"I am sure that Signor Starace will find it in order if in addition to himself a German representative accompanies Frau Scholtz-Klinck."

I was going beyond my brief, but the situation seemed to call for some intervention. Being unable to suppress their laughter one or two of the German officers had disappeared into the next room. Von Mackensen was grinning.

"Of course, of course," he put in.

But Starace's southern temperament got the better of him and he drew himself up indignantly.

"May I ask if my person is not sufficient guarantee?" he demanded fiercely.

"Of course it is," I said soothingly. "There is not the slightest doubt about that, but you must remember, Signor Starace, that Frau Scholtz-Klinck is on an official visit from the German Reich and therefore it really is appropriate that wherever she goes she should be officially accompanied. It seems to me that in the present instance the presence of the German Ambassador, Herr von Mackensen, is indicated."

Von Mackensen smiled again.

"Why, of course, Herr Dollmann is right. Don't you agree, Signor Starace?"

There was nothing Starace could do but swallow his anger and pretend to agree that, indeed, I was right.

"Of course," he said curtly. "Of course."

With that the gilt was off the gingerbread for Starace. Frau Scholtz-Klinck did visit the camp, but in the company of von

Mackensen, and only for an hour or two in the afternoon. There was no tent vigil.

A day or two later I was passing the time in a cinema. I was bored and the film was boring. I had been to the cinema so often lately. There was so much time to be disposed of. And suddenly I had a feeling that someone had put a hand on my shoulder. In a panic I leapt to my feet in the middle of the performance and blundered along the row, treading on people's feet and ignoring shouts of "Sit down!" Outside I was bathed in sweat. It was pure imagination on my part. There was no policeman. But in view of what soon followed I am beginning to believe in premonitions. When I got back I flung myself on my bed quite shaken and swore never to go into a cinema again —at least not until I could do so with impunity. But a week later—it was November 7th—I broke my vow. I really don't know why. Perhaps because, after all, the cinema was one way of passing the time and I had almost exhausted all the others. In any case, after an afternoon's walk I found myself in front of a little cinema showing a film called "Kisses you dream of." It was the cinema in which I had experienced my strange foreboding the week before. I bought myself a ticket and went in. There I sat and watched the kisses you dream of. But I had a rather disagreeable feeling running up and down my spine. I had seen two of the promised kisses when once again I felt a hand on my shoulder.

I had already decided to go and see a specialist when a firm voice whispered:

"Kindly leave the cinema with me."

It wasn't imagination this time. At least it would save me the doctor's fee. I got up and went out quietly, closely followed by a clearly recognizable type in civilian clothes.

"What's the meaning of this?" I demanded, but I already knew that it was a silly question. I knew perfectly well what the meaning of it was. The man promptly produced his authority and unnecessarily informed me that he was a detective officer. Waiting close by for us were two armed carabinieri. Then I remembered my American papers and I produced them with a greater show of indignant confidence than I felt.

"It's no use, Signor Dollmann," said the detective. "We know perfectly well who you are. You must come with me."

However, I continued my bluff and pushed the identity card under his nose.

"I don't know what you're talking about," I said firmly. "My name is not Dollmann but Alfredo Casani. Here: you can see for yourself."

The man took the identity card unwillingly, looked at it doubtfully and was obviously impressed by the fierce-looking American eagle on it. Then he looked at me.

"I'm sorry," he said, "but you must come with me. If I am mistaken it can all be cleared up quite easily at the station."

With that he nodded to the two carabinieri, who closed in on me and there was nothing to do but go with him to the police station. The officer in charge looked at my false identity card, and he too was obviously impressed, but he had a brilliant idea.

"We'll get into touch with the Americans at once," he said, "and if they send an officer to vouch for you, you can go."

I felt quite confident at this as I thought of my American friends Jim and Joe. Once again I placed my trust in Americans, and once again I was let down. Instead of an officer, a G.I. arrived, and a Negro at that. The Americans seemed to attach very little importance to me and that stiffened the Italian's attitude.

"I'm sorry, Sergeant," he said, amiably promoting the Negro a grade or two, "but I need the authority of a commissioned officer. I shall have to send Signor . . . Signor Alfredo Casani (reading the name from the identity card) to the Presidium. Everything can be satisfactorily cleared up there."

The Negro shrugged his shoulders and departed without protest. He wasn't much interested in me. The two carabinieri were grinning now and without more ado they took me out to a waiting jeep and we all piled in and drove off at speed to the Police Presidium, a large and gloomy building I knew well. It looked just the same as it had looked ten years before, and would no doubt look ten years after—"Police" it said grimly. No one could possibly have mistaken it for anything else but police headquarters.

I was put into a room with a plush sofa and two plush arm-chairs. The one table there was of wood, but only, I'm sure, because you can't make tables of plush. Round the walls were photographs in horrible gold frames: the portraits of all the Police Presidents of Rome since the year dot.

They kept me waiting there a long time and I walked up and down the room under the eyes of the former Police Presidents. Getting tired of walking I stopped and studied one of them. It was old Palma, who had been Police President under Mussolini. He looked a harmless old buffer, a grandfather with pince-nez glasses. But I knew better. Whilst I was looking at him his successor entered the room. I knew him too. It was Polito, a short, dark-haired type. Under Mussolini he had been out of a job. One of his first jobs after Mussolini's fall was to escort the Duce in a police waggon, during which he whiled away the time by telling Mussolini of his illegal activities to overthrow the Fascist regime.

"Ah, so there you are, Signor Dollmann!" he exclaimed with mock amiability.

I had determined to play my role to the end.

"I beg your pardon," I said firmly. "My name is not Doll-mann, but Casani—Alfredo Casani."

And once again I put my false identity card under an Italian policeman's nose. I still hoped that at the last moment the Americans would intervene and fish me out of the soup. The Police President took the identity card, looked at it and then flung me a nasty look, obviously angry at the waste of time the little deception involved. Without a word he then went out taking my false identity card with him. I was again alone with the former Roman police worthies and the dusty plush furniture. That identity card was obviously a stumbling block to them and I had not yet given up all hope of the Americans. But then the door opened again, and when I saw who it was this time I knew the game was up.

I knew him too, and he knew me. It was a man named Alienello who had served during the German occupation as a sort of liaison officer between the Italian Police and the German Security Service in Rome under the S.S. Leader Kappler. The two had got on well together, and Alienello had used all his widespread official and unofficial connections to make life pleasant for his German colleague. As his pal Kappler hated me and did his best to make things difficult for me, so Alienello had followed suit until Bocchini had sharply put him in his place. This must have been a real moment of triumph for the little rat.

"Oh, good afternoon, Herr Oberst Dollmann," he said, and he gave me a greasy smile as he bowed.

I could have spat in his face, but I made no reply and turned away to study old Papa Palma again.

He came round beside me.

"How are you, Herr Oberst? Is there anything I can do for you? Is there anything I can get for you?"

I rammed my hands in my pockets, ignored him and went on studying the features of Papa Palma. After a while he gave it up and disappeared. After that I was alone again for a while. In the next room I could hear Polito ringing up various people about me. But he didn't seem to be doing very well, for he was growing angrier and angrier, and the angrier he grew the more he raised his voice, and the more he raised his voice the better I could hear him. Finally he was speaking to someone who, to judge by the rude and bullying tone he adopted, must have been his wife.

"What!" I heard him shout. "Birthday party? Don't be a fool. I can't be bothered with birthday parties. That damned Dollmann of all people has just turned up." For a moment or two he was silent. No doubt his wife was getting a word or two in edgeways. Then I heard him shriek: "Spaghetti! I don't care if it will get spoiled. Take it off then. No! I can't help it if this fellow Dollmann turns up. Yes, of course it's Dollmann. That is, I think it is. What? For heaven's sake, woman! Leave me in peace."

And with that he banged down the receiver. For the first time I grinned to myself. After that the telephoning went on. In the meantime no doubt Signora Polita had taken off the spaghetti. It seemed to be her husband's birthday; I was the rather awkward present. Whenever he was talking officially I could hear his tone drop and he spoke with reasonable politeness, but whenever he was talking to anyone he knew, particularly anyone who congratulated him on his birthday, he nearly went through the roof about me.

Whilst Polito was personally conducting his inquiries and making arrangements for his spaghetti to be put on the hob, I was visited amidst my plush and photographs by various police officials, *Commendatori* and *Cavalieri*, I had known from the old days under Mussolini. Their masters had changed, but they, like Italy herself, seemed not to have changed; they still held down their jobs. The news of my presence must have got around. They all seemed anxious that I should make my escape. They even promised to help me. There was, it appeared, a subterranean way out of the Presidium.

I refused to play. There was nothing I would sooner have done than make my way through that subterranean passage to freedom, but I didn't know whether I could trust them. Their readiness to help me might be a trick. If it was and I agreed to their proposals then it would be clear beyond all doubt that I was Eugen Dollmann and not Alfredo Casani, so I kept up my blank front. I looked at them coolly and pretended not to know any of them.

"Mistaken identity, gentlemen," I insisted. "Before long I shall be released. Thank you for your kind offers of assistance, however."

In the end they all went off shaking their heads. At least they had to admit to themselves that such reserve was not in the least like me.

In the meantime I had heard two names on the telephone: one of them sounded hopeful and the other depressing. Although Polito uttered them both in a tone of reverence, he was so excited that his voice was still loud enough for me to hear them quite clearly. The first name was Gullo. That was the unpleasant one. Now as far as I could see there were two ways in which I could hope to be rescued from this dump. One was that the Communists might get me out, and the other was that the Americans might. Once the name of Gullo was mentioned the former possibility seemed very unlikely. Gullo was Minister of Justice in the fourth post-war Italian Government and a fanatical Communist. It was therefore extremely unlikely that his fellow Communists would do anything to upset him.

Whether the Americans would come forward and stand by their document issued to Alfredo Casani began to look more and more doubtful.

But a third possibility was implicit in the second name mentioned: de Gasperi. I knew Gasperi. He had once been an Austrian deputy for the Province of Tridentino, or Trient as it was then called. As such he had always bought his cigars and his tobacco from Bibi's mother in Trento, or Trient. The mother of the present Princess Ruspoli had always been an enthusiastic admirer of the "typical Austrian", as she had called him; at least he spoke perfect Viennese German. He was an anti-Fascist of course, and he spent part of his time in Austria and part in Italy. When Italy entered the war he disappeared behind the walls of the Vatican. During the war, whilst both the Germans and the allies were showering bombs on his homeland, he spent the time in praying and attending to his duties as a subordinate official in the famous Vatican Library. After the war he came out of his hiding place as a new type of martyr and entered the political arena once again. Before long he was Premier. I had some reason to hope that he might be favourably inclined towards me because it was I who, at the suggestion of the Fascist Chief of Police, Bocchini, had left him in peace in the Vatican and concealed his presence there from the Nazi authorities in Berlin, a circumstance of which he must have been aware.

Whilst I was engaged in weighing up all these rather complicated pros and cons the door to the Police President's room was suddenly opened by a carabinieri and a polite, familiar American voice called out: "Come in, please."

I went in. Behind the large desk of the Police President sat that gentleman himself, still looking very hot and bothered, between my old friends Jim and Joe of the American O.S.S. The two American angels were chewing away and smiling amiably. Against the wall was a carabinieri holding my British military rain-coat in one hand and my rather battered felt hat in the other. Polito was the first to speak:

"My dear Dollmann, why on earth did you have to choose just my birthday to go and see that film about the kisses you dream of? You've caused quite a lot of confusion."

I bowed formally.

"I hope Your Excellency will accept my apologies," I said. "I was unaware that it was Your Excellency's birthday."

That seemed to strike both Jim and Joe as the very cream of humour and they leapt to their feet roaring with laughter, and taking me each by one arm and paying no further attention to Polito they led me out of the room and down to their waiting car, apparently highly satisfied at their personal victory over the Italian police. They put me in the back of the car, pushed a couple of packets of chewing gum into my hand and then climbed into the front and drove off, talking hilariously.

It was raining in torrents and the drops ran down the window panes like pearls. When I got back to my own apartment it was cold and disagreeable. Outside the rain was still pelting down. Jim and Joe had left me down below. I was just where I had been before. Bored and fed up.

CHAPTER V

IRON CURTAINS

OUTSIDE the drawn blinds of my room the rain was still pouring down. My blinds were no longer of curtain material but of iron. I had exchanged my private quarters with its sexual library for a small and gloomy cell in the American military prison in Rome. Even apart from that I wasn't feeling too cheerful. There was iron, iron and still more iron all around me, and beyond the iron there was rain. I sat on my hard American field-bed and looked through the iron door, actually it was a gate. Through that I could see another iron gate, and through that a third one. Beyond the third one was a cold and narrow corridor. Just under the ceiling there was a thin slit which older prisoners declared was a window. Having nothing else to do I had already spent two days trying to decide whether that wretched slit could properly be called a window, and in the end I came to the conclusion that as a result of their long stay in prison the older prisoners had just lost all idea of what a window really was. Putting it at its best, I should have called it an air-hole. Ten days previously I had been brought through that corridor past the air-hole by military police and lodged in the cell I was now occupying behind the three iron gates. When I think of the circumstances that brought me there I get wild even now.

When Jim and Joe dumped me in my old quarters after rescuing me from the hands of the Italian police I fell on my bed and went to sleep at once. I was awakened the next morning by the ringing of the door bell. Putting on Bridge's rain-coat, which I used instead of a dressing-gown, I went to the door. There they were, the pair of them. I wasn't feeling particularly cheerful, for one thing it was still raining, but they were on top of the world. They burst into the room, sat down as though thoroughly exhausted in armchairs and, of course, put their feet on the table. Then they poured out all the news they had read or heard of—concerning me of course. They had brought piles of newspapers with them, Italian and others, and in all of them my name was on the front page complete with disagreeable commentaries and awkward questions. "What is Colonel Dollmann doing in Rome?" one of them wanted to know. "Hitler's Italian agent in American hands" another informed its readers. Jim and Joe assured me that I was quite safe, but I was not altogether confident. I didn't like the sound of it all in the least.

And my feelings in the matter were well founded. A few days later they arrived with more newspapers and the disturbing news that I was not so safe after all: they could no longer guarantee to protect me here. It appeared that the big Communist bosses had put their foot down. The previous night Moscow radio had announced that "the notorious Colonel Dollmann" was living in a luxurious villa in Rome under the protection of the American Secret Service. 'What the hell's so notorious about me?' I thought But there was worse to come: the American State Department had taken the matter up. Perhaps they intended to hand me over to the Russians? The idea was absurd really, but it seemed quite real to me at the time, and my misgiving was strengthened by the strangely uncertain behaviour of my two Mutt and Jeff protectors. They were both anxious to assure me that I was quite safe—well, not exactly quite safe perhaps. In fact my situation was on the whole rather dangerous. In the end their feeble assurances turned out to be an introduction to the news that they were now pulling out of the whole affair and leaving me to the mercies of someone else.

The following day they both appeared again, dressed in black rain-coats—it was still raining—and "requested" me to follow them. They assured me that they were taking me to a safer place, a villa outside Rome. I rather distrusted Americans by this time and I didn't know whether to believe them or not, but there was nothing else to do so I went with them. Down below we got into their car and raced off towards the Tiber. It was yellow and swollen from the rains and its banks were wet and slimy. Then the car stopped and another car pulled up behind

us. Jim and Joe then informed me that as they were not allowed
to operate outside the town I should have to get into the other
car. There was a rather fat man in it and not a particularly
agreeable type. He was introduced as Major Pagnotta, the Vice-
Chief of the American C.I.C in Rome. He didn't seem to care
much for me either and he treated me as though I were a pretty
low sort of criminal. He explained rather unwillingly that the
villa outside Rome to which I was to go was not yet ready to
receive me and that I should therefore have to spend the night
in the American military prison. It sounded all very unconvincing, but there was still nothing I could do about it, so off
we raced. At the prison I was delivered into the hands of a
couple of military police officers and they escorted me through
the long, dismal corridor with the air slit, through three barred
gates, and into a cell. When he departed Major Pagnotta still
insisted that it was only for one night—on his word of honour,
he said.

For a week I had been incarcerated there, complete with an
American Major's word of honour, but without light and without being able to leave the cell after dark to attend to any little
human necessities that arose. Major Pagnotta, it seemed, had
issued orders that no prisoner was to be allowed out of his cell
after dark to go to the lavatories. After long shouting and banging which went unanswered the unfortunate prisoners had
finally to use anything that came to hand, for their distress
was dire. Shaving mugs for example. This seemed to convince
our American gaolers that we were barbarians on a very low
level of personal hygiene.

One day—though it might well have been in the night, I
had no satisfactory means of judging—I heard a clinking and
a clanking at the first iron gate, and then at the second, and
finally at my own. I had heard it all half asleep and I made
no attempt to move.

"Get up!" someone shouted.

I slowly opened my eyes and took my time, and the voice
bellowed the order again. A torch was shining on me and with
some difficulty I rolled off the hard steel laths of the U.S. Army
field-bed and got to my feet. At that moment the lights went
on in the cell and in the corridor, and there I stood in shirt

and pants, rubbing the sleep out of my eyes. There were my two police officers, one or two obviously high American officers and then a man who looked as only an American General can look: a man with a face like leather in a uniform. No need to describe him further, the type is fairly common. My type seemed to be less common, for they all stared at me as though I were a tramp in a doss-house, which is, I suppose, just what I did look like in the circumstances, which were such that I would defy anyone to look any different in them.

When he had looked his fill at me the General barked sharply: "I am General Lee."

"Oh, yes," I said, and nodded. There seemed little else to say. At that time General Lee was in command of the U.S. armed forces in the Mediterranean. A little later on he was deprived of his command for some reason or other and sent home. Unfortunately at the moment he was in my cell looking at me as though I were some strange animal.

"So you're Colonel Dollmann," he said.

"I am," I said. The time for denying it had long passed.

"The capitulation colonel, what!"

This he seemed to find very witty, for he laughed heartily. I was interested only in interrogations which looked as though my release might be somewhere at the end of them. This one —if such it could be called—didn't, and all I wanted to do was to lie down again and go to sleep. He had nothing hopeful to report.

"You're staying here," he said.

I thought of inviting him to inspect the nightly lavatory arrangements—a shaving mug in my case—but with that he turned about and stalked off, followed by his suite. One by one the iron gates were locked behind him and I went back to my hard bed to dream of light, sunshine, and lavatories a man could use just whenever he wanted to.

During the next three months nothing at all happened, at least, nothing happened to me. I didn't see General Lee and his gentlemen again, and the only human beings I did see were the two American warders. One of them was some sort of a half-caste and the other had been a street sweeper in New York. Every night they both seemed to enjoy themselves hugely consoling the disturbed prisoners with the thought that they'd be able to go the next morning.

The amount of water they provided us with to wash in might have been enough for a family of cats, but for human beings it was inadequate. I was never allowed out for exercise and the only walking space I got was in my cell. However, my fellow prisoners—former military police who had been divested of their authority for various crimes—had less cause to complain. All day long they were taken out of their cells and put through the hoop in the passages: "Knees bend! Knees straight! Knees bend! At the double on the spot! Pick 'em up! Pick 'em up!" Until they must have been fit to drop. Whilst all this was going on I would lie in my cell and listen to it. I thought the barrack-square mentality was supposed to be purely Prussian; those Americans had it all right.

Three times a day I saw a human face. It wasn't a very pleasant face, but at least it was human, and that was when the half-caste pushed my meals through the hatch—American Army rations. For the rest, it rained all the time—three months on end. As far as I was concerned life seemed to have come to a stop.

Then at Christmas things brightened up a bit. A party of German prisoners was brought in. They were men who had escaped from various prisoner-of-war camps and been recaptured. There was no room for them in the cells so they had to park themselves in the corridors where they were guarded by warders. I tried to get in touch with them, and that evening, when supervision became a little less watchful, I succeeded. The man I spoke to promised to let the Vatican know of my plight. He probably never did, but at the time his promise cheered me up no end, made me feel patriotic, and produced something like the Christmas spirit. The carols of my fellow countrymen in the corridors did the rest. That evening imprisoned soldiers of one army celebrated Christmas with arrested military police of another, fraternising and carolling away in a foreign country at the tops of their voices. Altogether it was a grotesque Christmas Eve.

After Christmas the subterranean silence descended on me again and the only sounds of life came from the unfortunate

American prisoners being put through the regimental hoop. The sounds were so familiar by now that they were a mere background; I no longer consciously heard them. At first various officers had visited me from time to time in my cell to inquire about this or that diplomatic finesse of the Third Reich, and on one occasion—it was shortly before Christmas—one of them had even escorted me into the upper world to make a statement concerning Marshal Kesselring, who was at that time being tried by some court or other. It was noteworthy as being the only occasion I have ever seen the dome of St. Peter's through the barred windows of a prison. It was still raining and the view was hampered by mist, but there it was, as solid and impressive as ever. A few minutes later I was taken away and buried once again below the level of the Tiber in my subterranean dungeon.

I had long ceased to count in days; it was weeks now, even months. Finally, when not a soul came near me, I began to feel sorry for myself. In one of my sleepless nights I came to the conclusion that I was a totally superfluous individual, otherwise all this couldn't have happened to me. What was the use of going on eating up the rations of the U.S. Army? I therefore decided to end my unimportant life. It wasn't easy. The technical preparations could be made only at night when no one bothered any more about the prisoners all safely locked in their cells. Incidentally, the conditions for ending life were not particularly favourable in the American military prison in Rome. The only things at my disposal were my bed, a small table, a chair, and the clothes I stood up in.

The belt of the rain-coat Major Bridge had given me would do in place of a rope, and, rather sadly, I removed it from its loops. Just under the roof there was an air-hole with two bars. If I made a loop at one end of the belt and fastened the other to one of these bars, that would do the trick. There was no difficulty in getting the loop round my emaciated neck, but to fasten the other end to the bar was a problem. Standing on the chair I couldn't reach up high enough, so I propped the chair carefully against the wall and tried standing on the back. I was much more afraid of falling down and breaking my neck than I was of hanging myself, but at last I worked out a method of reaching the bar. Rome was celebrating carnival at the time, and the thought didn't improve my spirits. But at least it did give me an idea about the day on which to end it all. Ash Wednesday, of course.

But before the dismal day dawned who should turn up unexpectedly in my little cell but Jim and Joe. Escorted by two warders they looked a bit sheepish when they greeted me, but they made up for it by their enthusiasm. You would have thought we were all long-lost brothers. When the greetings were over—they were not quite so enthusiastic on my side—Joe pulled a wad of notes from his pocket and handed them to me.

"What's that for?" I demanded, because it was not yet clear to me what I was to do with money in my situation.

"It's five hundred Swiss francs," Joe explained, and in the meantime Jim examined my cell curiously.

"What's the use of five hundred Swiss francs to me?" I exclaimed irritably. "You should have brought me some closet paper. That would have been more useful."

"Oh, Mr. Dollmann!" exclaimed Joe reproachfully.

"Never mind about 'Oh, Mr. Dollmann!'" I exploded angrily. "What are you trying to do? Pull my leg? Can't you see what a state I'm in? What am I supposed to do with this blasted money? Why, I can't even tell down here when the sun's shining."

In view of this inhospitable outburst Jim and Joe retreated to the door, where they waved to me and disappeared through the succession of iron gates, having wished me "All the best". By that time I was pretty near the end of my tether and it wouldn't have taken much to make me burst into tears.

"All the best!" I repeated to myself bitterly and I sat down on my bed. My glance fell onto Bridge's rain-coat, and in particular the belt. That was the best I could think of. The world was rotten, and my world in particular. I therefore decided that I would leave it that very evening—with Joe's five hundred Swiss francs in my pocket.

When silence gradually fell in the prison I started on my much-tested preparations. I made as little noise as I possibly could, for I wanted to do my dying without interruption. I propped the rather wobbly chair against the wall under the air-hole. I had rehearsed it often enough; this was to be the real

111

thing. Having done so I sank down on my bed again feeling quite exhausted. It wasn't that the chair was at all heavy, or that any special effort was necessary to prop it into position, but suddenly I felt the injustice of it all. After a while, during which I had quite pointlessly contemplated the terrible end the world must come to—what did it matter to me, anyway?—I got up, and inwardly wrestling with my own decision, I climbed onto the chair and tied the belt to the bar and put the already prepared noose round my neck.

And there I balanced precariously in my pants and shirt. It was a solemn moment. Just before death all the beautiful scenes you have ever experienced in your life float kaleidoscopically before your eyes. I knew that. But with me they didn't. That was the first thing that went wrong. All I could think of was the iron bars in the air-hole up above me, the three iron gates that barred the way to freedom, and the faint shimmer of light visible in the corridor. That wasn't a beautiful picture at all. My failure caused me to go into everything again, but I still came to the conclusion that very few people had had such a raw deal as I had. Fortified by this conclusion I summoned up my courage and kicked away the chair from under me.

For perhaps the tenth part of a second I started to die, but at the end of it I found myself lying on the stone floor of my cell with a terrible pain in my knee where it had broken my fall. The belt of Bridge's rain-coat was still round my neck, but where it was fastened to the bar it had given way.

This filled me with patriotic contempt for Allied military tailoring—a German belt would have done the job. But this feeling was immediately superseded by the pain in my knee which made me so angry that I determined never to try to commit suicide again. The attempt could obviously be very painful. Then I experienced a sudden feeling of courage and confidence; no doubt a feeling of relief at finding myself still alive, but which I interpreted as a higher sign that in return for all my good deeds I was to be left alive. At which I fell back onto my hard bed in the American military prison of Rome in mingled physical pain and moral confusion and finally slept to be wakened up only by the stinging smart as an American first-aid man applied iodine to my bleeding knee. By this time all thoughts of suicide had gone for good and I felt rather glad that British belts weren't as good as German belts. If they were I shouldn't be here to write my memoirs now.

For days after that I spent the time lying apathetically on my bed, occupying myself with nothing, not even with myself, which, for one who had just returned from the dead, means something. I ate very little and I found myself chewing my corned beef to the rhythm of the shouting outside in the corridor as the American prisoners were put through their daily dozens. I don't know why I remember it so clearly, but this particular corned beef was canned by Mayer & Co., of Chicago, U.S.A. and it was "the best in the world".

Easter came, and it was no time of hope in our prison. Everything was just the same as before and nothing happened—certainly not my release—but soon after I fell seriously ill. Probably the fact that for six weeks I was not allowed to leave my cell at nights to attend to my natural impulses had something to do with the kidney trouble that developed, plus the fact that I was never allowed out into the air and the sunshine —when there was any—but was forced to stay the whole time in a damp, underground cell.

I had never been so ill in prison and I lay there on my hard bed, groaning and from time to time calling out for attention, but no one took the slightest notice of me or my condition. The cell was so damp that on the walls there was a flourishing crop of fungi surrounded by a field of mould. After a week of this someone seems to have noticed that I was still alive, for a medical officer came to see me. He was like a being from another world—which is not surprising, because that is precisely what he was. He wore a beautifully cut uniform and white gloves and he smelt of perfume, or it may have been hair oil. In his hand he carried a neat little medical case of suede leather. The first thing he did on entering my cell was to put his handkerchief to his nose.

"I can't treat you here," he observed with distaste. "No, certainly I can't treat you here."

He remained about three feet away from me, but I could smell his pomade, and to judge from the handkerchief he could smell me too. Cautiously he came just a little closer.

"What's the matter with you?" he asked. "I'm afraid I can't do anything for you here."

I didn't care a damn where he helped me as long as he did help me, but all he did was to open his little leather case and take out a little box, which he tossed onto my bed. To do this he had to put his handkerchief away, so he screwed up his nose instead.

"Take those tablets," he said. "They'll do you good. They're sleeping pills."

And with that the perfumed young lieutenant left me with the sleeping tablets, the fungi and my pain, and disappeared. I don't want to do him an injustice. Someone must have arranged for me to be taken out of my cell for examination, and he probably did. After I had slept for about three days—at least the pills did work—I was fetched by a horrified looking officer. He looked as though he thought I was going to die at any minute. But if I had died, one of the players in the Italo-German drama would have been lost. Perhaps I was still needed for a report to the American State Department—or perhaps it was just an article in the *New York Times*. In any case, something was done for me.

Apart from the danger of dying there was apparently also the danger of escaping, and to counter this he handcuffed me to a stolid American sergeant. Now I had been a prisoner for a good while and in a good many places by this time, but this was the first time anyone had handcuffed me. It was the last straw. I hardly realized what was going to happen, but when the cold steel clicked round my wrists I went mad, not as a matter of deliberate tactics but because something really had snapped.

"What do you think you're doing?" I shrieked.

"Handcuffing you," he replied drily.

"It's disgraceful," I shrieked. "I am an officer and I'm a sick man. If you don't know how an officer's entitled to be treated you can't handcuff sick men."

"I'm responsible for you," he replied coolly. His imperturbability made me more furious than ever. By this time I was in a frenzy and struggling fiercely. The huge sergeant remained as calm as his officer and made no attempt to restrain me although I was dragging him around furiously in a sudden access of strength I would hardly have credited myself with. Then, as quietly as ever, the officer unlocked the handcuffs and removed them, after which I calmed down and allowed myself to be taken upstairs without further resistance.

"Upstairs" for us meant light. But it was artificial light I was to get mostly, and far too much of it. In a room brilliantly lit with strip lighting I was put on an examination table—right under the glaring lights. I tried to turn my head away and I was sweating like a bull and wishing myself back in my cell again. And very quickly I was. The examination was very short and then I was taken down into the basement again and put into my cell, but in the meantime I had been provided with clean linen. There I lay exhausted and waited for what was going to happen next.

What happened was another visit from General Lee and his suite. The only difference was that this time I was lying down and he seemed to have grown fatter.

"Well, Mr. Dollmann," he said, "how are you?"

"You can see how I am," I answered bluntly. It struck me as a damn silly question. He took no offence.

"How have you been treated here then?" he wanted to know.

I told him about the refusal to let us out of our cells at night to go to the lavatory, about the refusal to allow me to take any exercise, or ever see day-light, about the primitive washing conditions and about the general callous neglect. He really seemed to be shocked and he began to bawl at the adjutant:

"That's incredible," he shouted. "How is such a thing possible?"

His adjutant and the officers with him probably had no more to do with it than he had but they all looked suitably sheepish and began to mutter: "Incredible! Terrible!" And after that they departed in a body leaving me alone in my cell.

A day or so later the young army medical officer came again. This time there was no need for him to put a handkerchief to his nose. My cell and I had both been cleaned up. He informed me that I was to be carried out on a stretcher.

"A stretcher?" I queried. "I know I'm ill, but I'm not too ill to walk upstairs."

"Well, it's really on account of the Communists."

"What have the Communists got to do with it?" I demanded.

"I'm afraid you don't understand," he said. His voice sounded like a nurse soothing a refractory patient.

"I certainly don't," I said, but I showed no irritation. I didn't like the smell of the fellow, but he seemed quite a decent sort.

"You're leaving Rome this evening," he informed me.

"Oh!" I said. I didn't even say I was glad to hear it; it all depended where I was going. I had learned to be cautious.

"Yes. You must pack your things and then you'll be carried to the plane on a stretcher."

"Why should I have to be carried to a plane on a stretcher?"

"Because it isn't necessary that the Communists should recognize you," he replied, and with that he went away and the three gates opened and closed behind him.

That afternoon I was fetched. In the plane I noticed that the course lay northward.

We landed on the Rhine-Mainz airfield at Frankfort. It was a little before Whitsun 1947. An ambulance was waiting for me and I was driven out to a suburb whose name I have forgotten. Although the future was still uncertain it was with a feeling of exaltation that I once again found myself on German soil after many years and a lost war. To all inquiries the Americans shrugged their shoulders, presented me with large quantities of cigarettes and tins of food—and drove me out to a prison for juvenile delinquents.

It was 1947 and a bad time for Germans. In distress any other people would have been drawn closer together in a greater solidarity, and I must say that was just what I expected of the Germans, but I seemed to have been abroad too long. Changes had taken place in the meantime. The first indication I had was the speech of welcome delivered to me by the prison officer I was handed over to:

"We're in favour of the Amis here; get that. Anyone who tries to escape from this place gets shot; get that. The Amis are the masters now and it's up to us to obey them. And that goes for you too; get that."

I got it perfectly well. I have always been very good at understanding what people want of me—the only thing is I often don't oblige them. This man was different: he did oblige.

Probably at the instructions of the Americans I was quartered in something between an ordinary room and a remand cell. It was furnished with a bed, a table, chairs and an old couch. Over the window was wire netting. The door was rarely locked, but the corridor outside was watched by a warder.

My presence in a prison for juvenile delinquents naturally did not go unnoticed—nor did the things I had brought with me: a whole case of food and cigarettes. The result was that the door was constantly opening to admit some half-starved youngster begging for something to eat. When I inquired why they were in prison the answer was always more or less the same:

"Not enough to eat and so you pinch what you can lay hands on. And if you're unlucky you end up here."

I gave them cigarettes and something to eat, but very often the door was dragged open and a warder would rush in, cuff the unfortunate youngster left and right before my eyes and drag him off to his cell. I was so indignant that at first I thought of complaining to the Americans about the treatment meted out to these boys, but I knew perfectly well that the Americans weren't interested in Germans—something the Germans never realize—and so I never actually complained. In any case, I wasn't there for long.

On Easter Sunday the door to my cell was suddenly opened and two warders came in and stood smartly to attention. At first I thought that my reputation had gone up in their estimation and I was about to ask them who had ordered them to do me such honour when from the corridor I heard typical American voices and the sound of girlish laughter. Much puzzled I waited to see what was going to happen now. The warders still stood there stiffly to attention until two huge Americans walked in and pushed them out into the corridor. In the meantime I stood with my back to the window and watched the scene, a little amused and just a little anxious. What now? I thought.

"Hullo, Mr. Dollmann," bellowed one of the Americans. "How are you?" And he advanced towards me with hand outstretched. Just behind him was a German girl who reminded me of a kitten. There was another American and another German girl standing in the doorway. They also shouted hallo and waved their hands.

117

Having learnt by dint of bitter experience to be mistrustful I half suspected that this particularly friendly performance was the introduction to something really horrid, but it appeared that I was wrong.

"Hullo to you," I replied. "What's it all about?"

"About?" repeated one of the girls. "Why, we're taking you out of here, Eugenio. That's what it's all about."

'Eugenio,' I thought. So they know my name. They must be up to something or the other. They weren't doing this on their own account. I didn't know any of them. I put a good face on it.

"That's fine," I said. "Where am I going to?"

The bigger of the two Americans laughed.

"Just a little Easter excursion," he said. "We're celebrating, and you're coming along."

I was gradually getting used to odd things happening to me, and this particular one seemed harmless. In addition, the two German girls weren't bad looking. Naturally, the Americans chose the best of everything. It wasn't quite clear to me whether it was an order, a request or an invitation, but regarding it as the last-named I didn't see why I shouldn't accept it. I have often been accused of a partiality for ambiguous situations and I certainly accepted this one. At the same time I had a very strong feeling that I would not be returning to the juvenile delinquents so I packed up a shirt or two and a toothbrush, took my small case—which had become rather shabby by this time owing to such frequent use—and took a seat in the back of the enormous Buick between the two girls, who began, for some reason not clear to me, to make a great fuss of me. Perhaps they thought I was some highly important Ami on a special mission. In any case, there it was, and it was "Eugenio" here and "Eugenio" there.

Before we drove off the Americans stood up in the Buick and flung cigarettes to the juvenile delinquents assembled in the courtyard to see us off. Whilst the lads scrambled for the cigarettes the warders stood there to attention saluting, but in their eyes I could see hatred and resentment—directed not against the Americans, but against the youngsters of their own race who were scrabbling for the cigarettes. It looked to me

118

as though the lads would be in for it as soon as our backs were turned and I felt a bit sick.

We set off through the lovely Main countryside until the Americans decided to halt in a little village in the vineyards. There sitting at a table in a pleasant garden we were served with good German local wine—a few cigarettes and a little money worked wonders. The girls sang German songs and the Americans sang their army songs, and before they were too drunk to appreciate it I told them the story of the capitulation. Incidentally, it was at this unexpected party that I heard for the first time that Germany was not, and never had been, the chief enemy of the United States; that it was the Soviet Union.

A few more litres of wine and the Americans began to make passes at the girls. By this time I had my work cut out not to slide under the table and stay there. However, before they were too far gone, the Americans seemed to remember that they had a job to do, so we all piled back into the Buick and set off again. The sharp wind restored me and by the time we arrived in Oberursel I had all my wits about me again. There we stopped in front of a large red brick building, which, as I discovered, the late Kaiserin Augusta Viktoria had once built to house Protestant lady teachers.

We all got out and then to my surprise they said good-bye, got back into the car and drove off, leaving me alone in the park before the Kaiserin Augusta Viktoria Institute without a clue. In this new ambiguous situation Tex appeared. Tex was an American sergeant from Texas, and no doubt his real name was different. He was in charge of the Institute and its occupants —no longer Protestant lady teachers as it turned out. He strolled up to me with a bottle of whisky under his arm, stopped in front of me, looked me up and down and then gave me his hand.

"Mr. Dollmann, I presume," he said amiably in a German that was almost free of accent.

"That's right," I admitted, and before I could ask him what it was all about he bowed, very much like a head waiter, and asked:

"And what can I do for you? Would you like a room with a balcony? Or perhaps a room overlooking the park?"

At first I thought I was still drunk and I made no reply, but the American was not in the least disturbed by my silence. He just took me by the arm in a friendly fashion and led me up the gravel path towards the entrance, talking all the time.

"Now I happen to have a very nice room facing south. I rather think you'd like that."

I rather thought so too, for almost any room without barred windows struck me as something I should like quite well.

"Yes," I said at last. "That sounds as though it would do nicely."

"That's better," he said. "Now at least you're talking. What about something to eat? Would you like a meal in your room?"

"A meal?"

"Well, I don't suppose you've had an evening meal yet, and my other guests have already eaten."

"Your other guests? What sort of guests?"

"Oh, you'll soon see. 'Outstanding cases' we call them. You know, their affairs aren't wound up yet."

"I see," I said. No doubt I, too, was an "outstanding case". There was no doubt that my affairs hadn't yet been "wound up".

"If you're not too tired, Mr. Dollmann," he went on, "I'd like to introduce you to Axis Sally this evening."

"What!" I exclaimed, "is she here too?"

It was more for something to say and to show an intelligent interest in the conversation than anything else. However, I had heard of Axis Sally, though I didn't know much about her.

"Yes, she's here," said Tex. "She's the lady of the house, so to speak. What could we do? We had to arrest her."

"Of course," I said. "Of course." By this time I was feeling very charitable.

At the door he handed me over to a bowing German servant, who led me up to my room. In the large and rather gloomy hall the great ones of another day hung there in their frames. There was Wilhelm II, of course, and, naturally, his consort Augusta Viktoria. Hindenburg and Ludendorff were there, and a number of others. Rather incongruously Katherine Hepburn was there too. She hadn't very much on and she had obviously been torn out of an illustrated calendar and hung up there with the rest, probably by Tex.

The institute had a huge, gloomy library containing the mental pabulum of orthodox Protestant lady teachers, including the works of Ottilie Aildermuth, Ludwig Ganghofer and Courts-Mahler. But there were also the collected works of William Shakespeare—no doubt as a Teutonic poet.

A meal was served in my room. The German servant who had showed me up was very polite and obliging: no doubt he had instructions to be.

"What sort of people are here?" I asked.

He bowed again, which made me think that he probably had some of my cigarettes in his pocket already.

"Oh, various gentlemen," he said vaguely. "Herr Hofer, for example, the former Gauleiter of Tirol. And then various Generals and Ministers, and the former President of the Reichsbank."

"Who, for example?" I persisted.

He bowed again.

"I'm afraid I've forgotten their names, Herr Dollmann."

He hadn't forgotten mine apparently. Then he bowed again and as I said nothing further he respectfully left the room. You might have thought from his behaviour that I was the master of the house.

That evening, when I was already in bed and feeling very comfortable—it was so long since I had slept in a good bed, and this was a very good bed—Tex arrived and routed me out to pay my respects to Axis Sally. He took me to her room and waited outside. It was only later that I learned why he preferred to stay outside.

In the room were the works of Shakespeare on a shelf, and round the walls were various theatrical costumes, and in front of a cheval glass a rather small and ethereal creature was rehearsing a scene from *Romeo and Juliet*. When I came in she turned round and stared at me with some astonishment. Then she raised her hand and came towards me.

"Don't tell me," she said. "Let me guess who you are."

I bowed and said nothing. I always make a habit of letting the ladies have their own way if possible, and in this case there was no reason to object. I was also rather curious to know whether the lady, whose exact age it was difficult to guess, would find the right solution. She put her lilac-powdered head to one side and looked me up and down.

"You have just come," she said. "Now there was someone expected to-day. So you must be that someone."

The logic of that seemed unassailable.

"And in that case you're Mr. Dollmann."

I bowed again.

"Right first time," I said. "How did you guess?"

With a wave of her delicate hand she indicated an ancient rococo arm-chair provided by the Kaiserin Augusta Viktoria and I sat down in it.

"I know everything," she said with a smile. "But do you know who I am?"

"Certainly," I replied, but she took no notice and proceeded to tell me who she was and all about herself. Naturally, her name wasn't Axis Sally. What it was I have forgotten. She was an hysterical but charming creature of Irish extraction—which probably accounted for a good deal—and American nationality, which accounted for her presence here. She had come to Berlin as a young actress a short while before Hitler had come to power. She was a Shakespearian actress and her favourite role was that of Juliet. Her ambition—no mean one—was to be *the* German Shakespearian actress, and she believed that the founding of the Third Reich would give her her chance. Everything now went as she had arranged in her intelligent little Irish head that it should go.

The attention of Joseph Goebbels was drawn to her. How far his intentions went I can't say, but that, in any case, was the start of her career as a German State actress. Like a good many Irish people she was already deeply sympathetic to the interests of the German people and now, via Shakespeare, her heart went completely over to the Nazis. When the war broke out she was enthusiastically on Germany's side and she became an active propagandist in the Nazis' interests. Goebbels could use a person like her and she loyally followed his instructions.

Equipped with a caravan and loud speakers and supported by a small troupe she toured the prisoner-of-war camps and tried to win their inmates over to the cause of National Socialism.

After America's entry into the war and the landing in France there were soon camps of G.I.s and their officers for her to work on. First of all she would stage Shakespearian plays and after the performances she would come down from the stage and operate at close quarters amongst the men. Acting under Goebbels's instructions she would tell them that really it was all a misunderstanding: they oughtn't to be there at all. The Americans weren't Germany's enemies. Not even Bolshevist Russia was Enemy Number One for Western European civilization. Enemy Number One was the President of the United States, Roosevelt, who was selling Europe and America to the Bolshevists. If the Americans wanted to remain Americans and uphold the American way of life and not become Bolshevists they must come over to Germany's side.

Now Axis Sally was certainly a charming young lady, but I don't think her propaganda had much effect. As far as I know there was no volunteer American Legion on Germany's side during the war. However, she did her best until the American troops arrived to release her captive audiences, and that put an end to her activity on behalf of the Axis. When the German collapse came Sally was in what is now the Eastern Zone, but a well-founded misgiving concerning the attitude of the Russians to her Shakespearian performances made her choose the lesser evil and make her way to the Western Zone. She therefore provided herself with a perambulator, put a doll in it, dressed herself up to look exactly like the wife of a Russian officer, and then pushed the pram calmly across the border where she promptly fell into the hands of the Americans—but by no means a repentant sinner.

She continued to treat her own countrymen as traitors to Western European culture and civilization, and when the Americans presented her with nylons and bottles of perfume she threw them back—quite literally—in their faces. Hence the discretion of Tex in staying outside the door—the lady's outbursts were no joke. Her attitude nonplussed the Americans and they didn't know what to do with her, so they put her in the Kaiserin Augusta Viktoria Institute together with all the other "outstanding cases", former Nazi *Gauleiter,* Generals and other doubtful cases, including me.

"Well," she said when she had finished her story, "what do you think of that?"

"I think it's astonishing," I said, and I did. But I was still more astonished when she informed me that I was just the man to play opposite her in her Shakespearian roles. A better Prince Hal than I should make it would be difficult to imagine, she said. I found it impossible to resist her blandishments and in the end I agreed, so the former *Gauleiter* and broken-down Generals had the pleasure of seeing me in leading Shakespearian roles opposite Axis Sally.

Tex hadn't been far wrong when he described her as the lady of the house. She dominated the place, and everyone in it had to do what she wanted: learn English for example and play bridge. All the old Generals would much sooner have played taroc, or even poker, but she insisted adamantly that bridge was the game for Western European society, and whether they liked it or not, all of them had to play it. Axis Sally was a born propagandist and she kept the house in constant activity. She propagated not only Nazi ideas, but the English language, Shakespeare and bridge. She was an amazing example of what the Irish can produce.

One day a certain Colonel Webb appeared in our Institute—incidentally it had been re-christened "Villa Alaska". Colonel Webb had once been in command of the American troops in Puerto Rico, and having been used to dealing with hot-blooded natives there perhaps the U.S. authorities thought he was a suitable man for dealing with Axis Sally. They were wrong. He adopted the already tried methods of perfume and nylons, but the results were no different. Sally just threw them at him and railed against President Roosevelt, who, she continued to declare, was a criminal and Enemy Number One of all decent people.

And then a commission of American gentlemen turned up to try us. They were, it appeared, members of the House of Representatives and members of a commission of the House. They invited me to dinner, and whilst I was eating tinned fruit one of them said:

"Tell me, Mr. Dollmann, would you like to do us a great favour?"

"Well, yes, though I suppose it would all depend on what it was," I replied cautiously.

"Oh, it's nothing very much," the man replied. "All you've got to do is just knock over an ink-pot for us."

"Just knock over an ink-pot for you?" I repeated in astonishment. I knew I wasn't drunk, and I didn't feel ill, but there was such an air of unreality about the request that I wondered whether I had heard aright. I had.

"Yes," confirmed the speaker. "That's right. Just knock over an ink-pot for us."

"Well, I don't mind if I do," I said finally, so when the meal was over they led me into a neighbouring room in which there was a table already prepared for the experiment with three large and virgin sheets of white blotting paper and an ink-pot standing in the middle.

"If you please," said the American, and he indicated the ink-pot.

I picked it up and then turned to the audience. The faces of the American deputies were very solemn and set. This was obviously a serious matter.

"Would you mind first telling me what it's all about?" I asked. "It sounds nonsense to me."

"It certainly isn't, Mr. Dollmann. It's a scientific method of investigating the human personality and discovering human aptitudes."

"Aptitudes for what?" I asked.

"Well, when you tip that ink out suddenly, shapes will form on the blotting paper and they will show us what you're best suited for."

I couldn't think of any intelligent comment so I said nothing further and upset the bottle with a sharp movement of the wrist. The ink poured over the blotting paper in a big pool. Perhaps there were significant shapes too, I can't say and I wasn't much interested, but the Americans all crowded round the table eagerly and began to study the ink patch.

"Aha, Mr. Dollmann!" exclaimed their speaker. "Now you've given yourself away to us." There was triumph in his voice and I am sure he was quite convinced that all this ink-spilling business was to be taken perfectly seriously.

"What do you mean?" I asked.

"Well, now we can see just what sort of a man you are and how we can best use you."

"Well, how can you best use me?"

"That of course you will never know. That will remain a secret in our files."

"Oh!" I choked and I had as much as I could do to stop myself from roaring with laughter.

"You see, Mr. Dollmann," he went on, "now you always thought yourself an intelligent man, didn't you?"

It was quite true, but I could stand no more and I left the room before I burst.

Perhaps inspired by this modern scientific method of psychological analysis I suggested to Axis Sally that we should found an astrological society. With the aid of an ancient encyclopaedia we chose thirty different historical persons and wrote their names down on scraps of paper. After that you had to guess which constellation they were born under. I was right three times: once with Queen Elizabeth, whom I rightly guessed as Virgo, and the other couple of times with the Empress Catherine of Russia and Maria-Theresa of Austria, both of whom I guessed to be Taurus, lady bulls, or cows.

The next day at midday we had a surprise we hadn't read in the stars. We were all sitting in the large dining-room of the institute under the portraits of Hindenburg, Ludendorff and company when the clock struck twelve and the door was opened by an American officer. Two figures came into the room, a tall powerful fellow and a small slim one. At first I didn't take much notice of them, but then I had a closer look at the bigger fellow. Surely I had seen him somewhere before?

They passed by us and went up the stairs to the upper floors and as they went by the bigger man said:

"Morning, Dollmann."

Then I realized who it was.

"Morning, Skorzeny," I replied.

And that of course, was his adjutant, Radl, with him; the two still seemed inseparable.

I had not seen him since 1943 and his famous exploits in

Italy and now here he was in the Villa Alaska, amidst whisky bottles and packets of cigarettes, telling the story of his heroism to credulous American soldiers. He also had to go and be vetted by Axis Sally, who discovered that he couldn't play bridge. There was no exception even for "the hero of the Gran Sasso". He had to learn, and there he sat, "the most dangerous man in the world", and learned to play bridge in a room of a Protestant lady teachers' home from a fantastic young Irishwoman of American nationality and Nazi beliefs.

When one of those high American officers whose job it apparently was to clear up our "outstanding cases" came to our institute I told him firmly that I proposed to write a letter to the American President.

"Oh, yes," he said, "and what are you going to put in it?"

"What am I going to put in it?" I repeated indignantly. "Why, that I don't want to spend the rest of my life in the Villa Alaska, of course."

That officer was exceptionally intelligent; he seemed to realize at once what I wanted and after dinner that evening he sat down with me at a separate table and as a result of our conversation soon afterwards I left the building in a car accompanied by two American officers. Behind us the back of the car was full of tinned foods, packets of cigarettes and bottles of whisky. They dumped me and the contents of the car in front of an ancient Bavarian villa at Tegernsee and then they went back to listen to more stories from their fairy-tale prince Otto Skorzeny.

Before ringing the bell I carefully arranged everything I had brought with me in an attractive pile, then I put myself into position, rang the bell, and waited. After a while I heard shuffling footsteps and an old and half-starved retainer opened the door.

"George," I said. "What are you doing here?"

"Serving the family, sir," the old butler replied in a tremulous voice, but there was a flicker in his old eyes as he saw my pile of good things.

"And what are you serving them, George."

"Potatoes and salad, sir."

"We'll alter all that," I said.

CHAPTER VI

ROSES IN SOUTH TIROL

"HERE's looking at you," said my friend Müller, a former
Major in the Luftwaffe and a recipient of the Knight's
Cross. I had known him in Italy, but now, on November
29th 1947, he was in civvies. He was no longer engaged in
arranging squadron flights, but in arranging what there was to
be arranged in those lean years in post-war Germany. The whole
thing was a mystery to me and I often wondered just what it
was business men arranged and organized, but I didn't worry.
I raised my glass and looked over the top at Müller's long but
well-fed face and answered the toast.

Müller was not out of the top drawer. He hadn't the social
cachet of my aristocratic relations and he didn't possess any
works of art. On the other hand he didn't live on half-frozen
potatoes and turnips. I had left the choice ambient of my
antiquarian relations with their royal Bavarian memories and
all the other memories of the one-time Bavarian upper classes
and now I sat opposite Müller—he wasn't even a von. When
I use the word antiquarian to describe the atmosphere of the
Tegernsee villa I mean it literally, for the owner of that villa
was a sort of grand seigneur amongst the antiquarians of Europe.
For example, Barbara Hutton had taken advantage of his
services for the furnishing of her fabulous house in Regent's
Park. It must have cost her a mint of money and I believe she
was only inside the place once.

In any case, my reminiscences of Tegernsee were soon exhausted. There were only two subjects of conversation in that
villa: one was the next meal and the other was the Russian
danger, and both were very painful. When the old butler had
worked his way through the supplies I had brought and the
household was back to potatoes and turnips I thought it time
to turn southward again to the sun and spaghetti. My resolution

was strengthened when it began to snow with real German thoroughness. That was why I was now drinking whisky with my old friend Müller.

"And so," I said, "as you know all about contacts—connections over the frontier, and so on—I thought I'd come to you."

"And so the Field Marshal turned to me. 'Muller' he said . . ."

My patience was now exhausted. Every time he had headed me off and evaded the subject like a man without a passport dodging a control point. I banged on the table.

"Now listen, Müller. Be serious at last. I've got to get over the frontier."

"You want to get over the frontier," he said incredulously. "I thought you had just come to visit me."

With that he stood up and looked out of the window at the vast mass of the Alps in the distance and pointed to a chink in the arrangements.

"You must go over through there," he said. "That's the best way."

"But I don't know the way, Müller. That's just why I've come to you."

He passed his hand over his chin as though he wanted to know whether he needed a shave or could leave it for a while.

"So you don't know the way!" He sounded very surprised. "But if you don't know the way and you haven't got a passport . . ."

That was the limit. I had had enough of Müller for the time being, so resolutely I got up, picked up my rucksack and was about to clear off when he detained me.

"You needn't be so sensitive, Dollmann."

I stopped in my tracks and turned back.

"If you want to go over the Alps I can give you a strong pair of airman's trousers and a pair of mountain boots. And then there's a fellow I know who can find his way about there as though it were his own back yard. I'll get him on the job. To-morrow you'll be in Innsbruck."

"Now you're talking," I said, and I sat down again and he poured out some more whisky. We drank a lot of whisky that night, so much that when the following morning I followed on the trail of a former N.C.O. in the Luftwaffe, now a mountain guide, I could hardly keep up with him and wasn't over-keen anyhow. Müller stayed down below, of course, but he saw me off enthusiastically and told me that all those who were caught without passports were sent back again the same evening.

"Chops for dinner," were his last words. "I'll put down an extra plate. So long!"

I grunted. I wasn't feeling so bright as he was, but there, he wasn't making an illegal crossing of the Alps. My rucksack was terribly heavy and getting heavier, but grimly I toiled on after my guide. Up above me he stopped between a clump of firs and waited for me to come up. When I got there at last he pointed out a building I could just see in the distance.

"That's the customs point," he said.

"In that case that's precisely where I don't want to go," I said a little irritably.

The man grinned. His name was Huber.

"It would be all right if you had a pass," he said.

"No! You don't say so!" I exclaimed in mock astonishment. "But damn it, man, that's the very reason I'm here because I haven't got a pass."

I was getting annoyed.

"I know that," he said imperturbably. "I was only just saying that it would be nice if you did have one. You needn't shout. They might hear you."

I took a deep breath and said no more. After all, he was doing his best to help me and it was no use taking it out of him because of the idiocy of State frontiers. For about another half an hour I clambered and stumbled over rocks with him and then he stopped again and declared that from this point I must go forward on my own. He pointed to a little inn we could see on the Austrian side of the frontier.

"You make for there," he said encouragingly. "They give you something decent to eat."

And with that he turned round and went back. I went on, forcing my way through branches and bushes covered with snow, and in the meantime the snow found its way through my boots, which were no longer water-proof, and I got colder and colder despite my efforts. More than once I hid myself quite unnecessarily in a bush for fear the customs officials were around, but in the end I made it.

When I entered the little inn the innkeeper's wife, a big Austrian in a dirndl skirt and with rather too much bosom, realized at once what sort of a traveller I was, but it didn't seem to bother her and she bustled around getting me a meal to the sound of guitar music from a group of woodmen there. On the walls were pictures of the Archduke Johann. The meal, bacon and eggs in the Austrian fashion, was good and there was plenty of it; when I had finished I smoked a cigarette and listened to the stories of the Archduke and his great love with which the landlady regaled all her guests. In the meantime my outer clothing was drying in front of the stove. What with the landlady's laughter and swaying ear-rings, the singing of the woodmen, the good meal I had just eaten and the pleasant aroma of my cigarette I was now feeling very well content with myself and my lot and quite certain that Austria was such a very agreeable country that nothing disagreeable could possibly happen to me in it. Müller could keep his chops. I shouldn't be back. I was right there.

Half an hour later I left the hospitable inn and the pleasant company, and, still in the best of spirits, I made a prudent detour to avoid the customs control point. Should I take a train from Rattenburg straight to Innsbruck, or should I stay the night in Rattenburg? I felt rather inclined to the latter, since I had done so well with Austrian inns so far. I wasn't to do so well with the Austrian customs officials. Whilst I was cheerfully on my way to Rattenburg who should I spot coming towards me with a carbine over his shoulder but a person immediately recognizable from his uniform as a customs official. Spotting me he was in no doubt as to what I was or where I had come from and he shouted a word which was beginning to apply more and more not only to me but to a good part of the population of this unhappy earth:

"Halt!"

I have never resisted the orders of the proper authorities and I didn't this time. I would very much have liked to for once, for this man in uniform inspired me with distrust. Not that it was altogether his fault; any sort of uniformed official inspires a man in my position with distrust. However, there was his carbine to consider so I halted.

"Where have you come from?" he asked, quite unnecessarily, for I am sure he knew everyone by name for miles around.

"Me?" I said, equally unnecessarily, and I wondered where on earth I might have come from.

"Yes, you," he said. "I'm talking to you."

Which was very obvious. I decided to tell the truth frankly. I couldn't see what else there was to be done.

"Germany," I replied.

"Thought so," he said. "Where's your passport?"

"I haven't got one."

"Thought so too. Where do you think you're off to?"

"I want to get to Italy."

"Italy, eh? Any idea how many want to do that? And without a passport. You're a German officer, aren't you?"

Some damned fool once told me that Austrians hate German officers so I lied.

"Oh, no! I've got something very different to do in Italy."

It was a mistake. My next chance of saying anything reasonable was when we got to Innsbruck prison. In the meantime a storm of hostility broke.

"Something very different, eh? Now that's fine! For the Americans I suppose? In that case you've just come to the right address I can tell you. We don't need your sort here. If you'd been a German officer I'd have put you on your way myself. I was in Russia. Fought against that lot. You, you dirty agent, working for such people. You're a traitor. That's what you are."

Still shouting angrily he drove me before him towards the control point, putting the butt of his carbine in my back when I didn't go quick enough for him. I ended up in the frontier police station of the Austrian Republic. The next few hours I spent alone in a cell and that evening I was brought out for examination. The examiner was an elderly gentleman who was lighting his pipe when I arrived. I have said previously that when they get to a certain age all Austrians begin to look like the Emperor Franz Joseph. This one might have been the Emperor Franz Joseph himself.

I sat down in a chair in front of his desk and when he had finished lighting his pipe and it was drawing easily he leant forward with a friendly smile and adopted a fatherly tone:

"Now my dear fellow I think we can settle all this very easily if only you're reasonable. Just confess straight away. It's much better that way. For you I mean."

"Of course I admit it," I said. "I couldn't very well deny it, could I? Right: I came over the frontier illegally, without a passport."

"Come, come," he said. "That's not what I'm talking about, you know that. Just admit you were the man and everything's going to be all right."

I was frankly puzzled, but as the questioning went on at cross-purposes in this way I began to get alarmed. What on earth was the old buffer getting at?

"I just don't know what you're talking about," I said. "I crossed the frontier illegally. Admitted; but beyond that there's nothing."

"Now, now," he said coaxingly. "If you admit it straight away you'll certainly get extenuating circumstances."

"I can't admit more than I've already admitted. What is it you want me to admit?"

"Now don't pretend you don't know. It won't do you any good. We can't help you if you remain obstinate, you know. Just admit you killed her."

I stared at him in horror. At first I thought he was making a bad joke, but one look into his puffy, bloodshot, good-natured old eyes was enough. He was perfectly serious. He was looking at me as though I were a naughty boy who had to be brought to see reason—for my own good.

"Killed her?" I stammered. "Killed who?"

"It's the sort of thing that can happen, we all know that. All you've got to do is to admit it honestly."

He spoke as though I'd dropped something and broken it and didn't want to own up.

"Killed who?" I repeated.

"Now don't be silly. You know who I mean. There aren't any others, are there? I mean the rich Swiss woman in St.

Johann. It doesn't matter much why you did it. Perhaps you needed money, eh?"

I leant back in my stool feeling quite exhausted and stared at him unbelievingly.

"Or perhaps it was a sexual murder?"

That capped the lot and suddenly I came to.

"What the devil are you talking about?" I bawled. "The last time I was in St. Johann I was eleven years old. You don't murder people at that age."

"I must beg you to calm yourself," he said reproachfully. "You won't help yourself by losing your temper."

"Listen," I went on angrily, "if you don't stop that murder nonsense I demand to be brought before the Public Prosecutor at once, you understand?"

He was still quite calm and fatherly.

"Why make all that fuss?" he wanted to know. "We can do it all quite satisfactorily here."

"Fuss!" I shouted. "Fuss! When you accuse me of murder."

"Well we've got proofs, you know."

"I'd like to see them."

"You've got one of them on your wrist right now," and he pointed to my gold wrist watch. "It's a Swiss watch, and a gold one; just like the woman's watch."

It was difficult to penetrate that unshakable calm. For him it was quite certain that I had murdered a rich Swiss woman in St. Johann and stolen her watch. There it was on my wrist. I just wasn't prepared to admit it yet. But I would. I was almost beginning to agree with him, but I knew that I had bought that watch ten years previously in Geneva.

"But of course," he went on, "if you prefer to make your confession to the Public Prosecutor you can."

He paused to re-light his pipe.

"But why be difficult? You can do it just as well here."

It was obviously pointless to argue with the obstinate old fellow. The only thing was to keep as calm as he was.

"No," I said. "I don't want to see the Public Prosecutor after all. Your country is occupied and you are no longer a sovereign power. I demand to see the French High Commissioner."

That upset the old man.

"So you're one of those, are you," he said disagreeably, and he got up and left the room without another word. After that I was taken back to my cell.

About an hour later I was brought back to him and then he informed me just as calmly that in the meantime he had discovered that I was not the man who had murdered the rich Swiss woman in St. Johann, which was, despite the ridiculousness of the charge in the first place, something of a relief.

The next morning, escorted by a young French lieutenant, for I was now in charge of the occupying power, I was delivered into Innsbruck prison. The place had once been an inn and in summer roses still bloomed in profusion in the garden. It had been a favourite spot for lovers, but the authorities had spoiled the love-nest by introducing iron bars. I have often noticed that if the authorities requisition a building they usually turn it either into a tax office or a prison. This one they had turned into a prison, and there was very little love left in it.

The French lieutenant escorted me through dank and gloomy corridors and several times I bumped myself in the dark against projecting stones, Finally he opened a door which seemed to lead into the old wine cellar. Round the walls were broken-down old benches and on them sat broken-down old figures with bushy beards, a proper collection of Barbarossas. Most of them were asleep and they were grunting and snoring.

"Who on earth are these people?" I asked.

The French officer shrugged his shoulders.

"No one in particular," he replied. "Robbers and a murderer or two . . . Oh, yes, and a few Nazis."

"And you want to put me in there?" I demanded incredulously.

"Why not?" he inquired without much interest, and with an elegant wave of his hand he invited me to go in. "Is there anything in particular you object to?"

"Yes, I can't stand beards."

"I'm sorry about that," he said, "but we're not allowed to let them have razors."

We were still standing in the doorway and one or two of the prisoners of a foreign power had woken up and were watching us in the half light through screwed up eyes. They didn't seem very interested either.

"No," I said with determination. "I'm not going in there."

"Why not?" the officer demanded, but not very firmly. "They won't hurt you. And if they try to, well . . . the warder's in the corridor."

"So, the warder's in the corridor, is he? Well, I don't care where the warder is, I'm not going in there amongst robbers and murderers. I haven't deserved that."

"I'm afraid I must remind you, Monsieur Dollmann, that we decide what you have deserved and what you haven't."

He was a little more energetic now, but so was I. I didn't like the look of those hairy robbers at all.

"At least you don't decide it personally," I said firmly. "The High Commissioner perhaps, so take me to him at once."

At that I could see that the young officer had become a little less confident and I pressed my point.

"You've no right whatever to put me in with such people," I declared. "It's monstrous."

"We've only got these large cells here," he objected almost apologetically.

"Listen," I said generously after my victory, "I don't want to be awkward, but haven't you got something better than this at least?"

"Well, there is another cell, but the Stern gang is in there."

"The Stern gang? Who are they?"

"They're Jewish terrorists. They've let off a bomb at the main railway station in Vienna."

There wasn't much more I could do. I had shot my bolt. In any case they sounded better than this bearded lot.

"All right, put me in with them then."

Then he took me to a light and airy cell which was even provided with a cupboard and I walked in amongst the representatives of the people my people had sent to the gas chambers. Against the cell walls were benches and four well-dressed men sat there. Their ages ranged from perhaps nineteen to forty and they were strong and muscular. They looked more like S.S. leaders than Jews. I said good-day and sat down on one of the benches and waited to see what would happen. Then I noticed that the lieutenant was still in the doorway.

"Let me introduce you," he said. "Gentlemen, I've brought you a very agreeable companion. Colonel Dollmann of the S.S."

Then he grinned at me maliciously and closed the cell door. 'The dirty dog!' I thought. 'This is going to be good.' Fortunately I was near a corner and I slid along the bench into it. But nothing happened. They just looked at me curiously but without hostility.

"Are you the Colonel Dollmann that arranged the capitulation?" asked the youngest of them after a moment or so.

"That's right," I said.

At that he came over to me, sat down beside me and offered me a Camel.

"Where did you get that?" I asked.

All four of them laughed and one of them opened the cupboard. It was packed with foodstuffs and cigarettes. It reminded me of the Villa Alaska.

"You needn't worry," said the young man to me. "We only throw bombs at the British. Our Rabbis look after us here."

"Your Rabbis?" I repeated incredulously. It struck me as odd that Rabbis should look after bomb-throwers and provide them with American tinned food and cigarettes.

"Yes. After all, we did it for Israel."

"Ah, yes, of course."

I knew that spirited young men were always doing wild things for their various countries and they usually ended up in prison. These imprisoned Jews offered me food and I gratefully ate it, for I had had nothing to speak of since the Austrian landlady's bacon and eggs. Odd things were happening to me, but this situation was one of the oddest: there I sat, a former Colonel of the S.S., and ate the food of Jewish terrorists who had thrown a bomb at a transport of British troops on its way to Israel, and we were all under French arrest in an Austrian prison.

They were nice Jews and before long we were all quite friendly. When we got talking about various things they wanted to know how the S.S. worked.

"I'm sorry," I said, "but I know less about that than you do."

137

"But you were a Colonel in the S.S.," said the Benjamin of the group in astonishment. "You must know all about it."

"I was only formally a Colonel in the S.S.," I informed him, taking an American cigarette which was kindly offered to me. "In reality I had nothing to do with the S.S. It was a sort of diplomatic rank."

"You needn't be afraid of us," the older man said. "We know who you are."

His insistence annoyed me. "I tell you I had nothing to do with the S.S. and its goings on," I said irritably.

Young Benjamin poured me out a glass of brandy. 'Jews look after each other,' I thought. 'Perhaps it would be a good idea to go to Palestine instead.'

"Perhaps you can tell us where the S.S. kept its lists," he suggested.

"What lists, for goodness sake? I tell you, I never had anything to do with the S.S. measures against Jews."

"No," said Benjamin soothingly, "not the lists of Jews who were arrested and killed. The Allies have those. We mean the lists of those Jews who betrayed other Jews."

It was difficult to convince them that I didn't know anything about any S.S. lists, but fortunately the time came for their prayers and the subject was dropped.

The next day I was tried and convicted of crossing the frontier into Austria illegally. It was all very solemn. The trial took place in the large baroque hall in which Maria Teresa had once called her Tirolese representatives together. To-day the flag of the Fourth French Republic was spread out there. I stood before the bench and up above me a bored French military judge tenderly held a fat chin in one hand and looked at me without interest. The whole tiresome business lasted an hour, then we all stood up, including the judge, and the strains of the "Marseillaise" were churned out from a gramophone record and the verdict was announced.

"In the name of the people . . ."

'What people?' I thought idly.

The sentence was thirty days imprisonment and I was to serve it immediately. 'That'll take me over Christmas' I thought as they led me away and the judge turned his attention to the next case: someone had been stealing wood from the Austrian State domains now under the control of the French occupation authorities.

Back in my cell the Stern gang had prepared a meal of corned beef and a bottle of white wine to celebrate my conviction. It was all very nice, but after that they came back to my supposed knowledge of the S.S.

"As you were with the S.S." the oldest of them began, "you're bound to know something about the latest weapons."

But I was already just a little bit tipsy and I sat there happily and hummed the "Marseillaise".

"What weapons?" I asked. The fact was that I didn't know anything about any weapons.

"The modern weapons of the S.S.," the man explained patiently.

At that point young Benjamin took up the negotiations.

"Listen," he urged. "You're bound to know something about the latest automatic quick-firing rifles. You know, the 32-round ones."

"Benjamin," I said pityingly, "if you only knew. The fact is I don't know anything about weapons. Not in my line at all."

The older man looked down at me contemptuously.

"But as a Colonel in the S.S. you must at least know all about the 7.35 with the double magazine," he said.

I shook my head, and Benjamin turned to his companion.

"The 7.35 hasn't got a double magazine," he said. "You're mixing everything up."

"I'm not," retorted the other angrily. "You've no idea why the 7.35 has an automatic safety device at the left side of the barrel . . ."

"That's got nothing to do with the double magazine," shouted Benjamin.

They were well away now, facing each other like two fighting cocks. I felt tired. It was getting on, and I lay down on my bed and let the Jews argue it out. I hadn't the faintest idea whether the German 7.35 had a double magazine or an automatic safety device on the left side of the barrel, or both, or neither—and I didn't care. I went off to sleep.

Now and again a Rabbi used to visit my fellow prisoners and

talk to them about the Talmud and its power for sustaining the Jewish people. I had nothing else to do so I listened carefully too. Thanks to my short imprisonment with Jewish terrorists I came out knowing more about the Talmud and more about the weapons of the S.S. than I had ever known before.

It was very near Christmas and I had another couple of weeks to serve. The Jews gave me addresses and invited me to visit them afterwards.

"I don't want to be pessimistic," I said, "but bomb-throwing isn't child's play. Who knows how long it will be before you get out?"

Benjamin slapped me on the shoulder jovially.

"Jews stay in prison only as long as it suits them," he said confidently.

Perhaps that was what gave me the idea, for when the French officer came in to our cell the next time I told him that I had an invitation for Christmas from my aunt in Innsbruck.

He looked at me in astonishment for a moment, but then seemed to think the remark wasn't worth any comment so he shrugged his shoulders, shook his head and went off. The Stern gang were much amused.

"Now's the time," said Benjamin. "Start shouting, hammer on the door, kick up a fuss."

I followed his advice. At least I got them to haul me before the commandant for indiscipline. He was a lively little man with a small, black moustache which he kept stroking as he glared at me.

"You have been making a noise," he said. "What's the meaning of it?"

"I have an invitation to spend Christmas with my aunt in Innsbruck," I said, "and it's very nearly Christmas now."

He stared at me for a moment or two with popping eyes, got up and strode up and down the room on his short legs once or twice, perhaps to gather his wits. Then he bawled at me in a much louder voice than I would have thought possible:

"Have you taken leave of your senses? You just want to get out. Just like that!"

Despite his loud voice I could see that he was flabbergasted and didn't really know what to say. He sat down again in his chair and stared at me as though he expected me to help him. I was quite willing to. In order to give him some excuse for letting me go—for after all he was only a subordinate as I had once been and he had to consider his superiors—I had worked out a little plan.

"You see," I explained, "if on December 24th at twelve o'clock a telegram doesn't arrive from me in Zurich saying that I am free a journalistic bombshell will burst which the Allies will find very disagreeable."

He stared at me incredulously and took a deep breath.

"What?" he said, as though he couldn't believe his ears.

I repeated what I had said and his obvious bewilderment gave me courage I badly needed.

"I have collected certain material," I went on. "It is all ready for publication now. It will be published unless I send a telegram in code."

The Frenchman mopped his forehead.

"It has to be in code. A pre-arranged message."

I waited for his answer, but he said nothing, just pressed a button and had me taken back to my cell. I felt very pleased with myself. I could see an elegant limousine of the French occupation army waiting for me that evening outside the prison. But Benjamin disagreed with me.

"No," he said. "They'll make you wait until the last moment, you see. At 24.00 hours on the 24th."

"But then you can be certain of it," added another member of the gang confidently.

But their confidence had the effect of making me doubtful and by the next day all my courage had oozed out of my boots and I felt that I had only succeeded in making my situation worse.

"If they make any inquiries about that telegram business I'm lost," I said to young Benjamin. "There's not a word of truth in it."

"That's just why they'll believe it," he said.

I didn't quite follow his logic, but he turned out to be right. On Christmas Eve at 23.00 hours the door of our cell opened. The Stern gang stood there silently but highly amused and pushed me forward. They had every right to be amused: their

141

theory had turned out to be correct. A French officer stood there with his hand at the salute and bowed.

"Monsieur Dollmann, the car is waiting for you outside," he said politely.

I nodded farewell to the Stern gang and proudly marched out of the cell. It wasn't exactly an elegant limousine which was waiting for me, but an ordinary Citroën. However, I decided it would do and I made no complaints. At the end of the journey I summoned up enough sauce to inform the French commandant that I could not send off the telegram in his presence.

"Its contents must naturally remain a secret."

"Naturally," he agreed. "Naturally."

I don't know what he was really thinking but after that they handed me over to the American liaison officer in Innsbruck with the information that within fourteen days I must be outside their zone. And so I spent Christmas with my Innsbruck aunt after all.

When I told the story to a few of my Tirol friends over *Knödel* and *Geräucherte* they offered to help me over the frontier into Italy.

"Can you ski?"

"No, I can't."

"Never had skis on at all?"

"Never had them on at all."

It was a shameful confession to make to men of the mountains. On the other hand, I now had connections with the American liaison officer. His name was Captain Bell, and we got on famously together. As he hadn't the faintest idea what to do with the ex-Colonel that had been dumped on his doorstep he asked me for advice. I told him I wanted to get over the frontier into Italy, and although he had not the slightest objection he didn't see for the moment how it was to be arranged. Something certainly had to be done, for the French were interested in my disappearance. They feared that if I didn't go the Austrians would take the matter up again and that they would then have difficulties with their own government via Vienna. We discussed the matter at length over a bottle of sherry. Captain Bell was liason officer and he therefore couldn't offend the French, didn't want to offend the Austrians and was anxious to be of service to me. It was altogether a very pretty problem.

In the end he got up and began to stride up and down the room. He was obviously thinking very hard. Then he stopped and turned to me.

"Mr. Dollman, I've got an idea."

The Americans often have ideas. I had already suffered from some of them, but I hoped that something would come out of this one, whatever it was.

"What sort of an idea?" I inquired.

Before answering he emptied his glass.

"The Italians," he said. "They're the right people."

"That's just what I think," I said. "That's why I want to get back to Italy."

"Good. Now listen: all Italians can be bribed."

"Not all," I said. I had had more experience in that particular matter than he had.

"Well, these Italians certainly can. They're customs men."

I wasn't feeling very well disposed to customs men, Italian or otherwise, so I merely nodded.

"They take empty trains back over the frontier and for a consideration they'll take anyone with them—hidden in the brake-house."

If I had known then exactly how I was to get over the frontier I would have set off for the nearest brake-house at once, but I didn't. And then Captain Bell's Roumanian girl friend butted in and spoiled the whole thing.

"But, darling, Mr. Ross is coming to-morrow. Perhaps he'll be able to suggest something."

"Of course," said Captain Bell. "Yes, we'll leave it until he comes," and with great relief he produced another bottle of sherry. He was only too glad to forget the awkward job of transporting an ex-Colonel of the German Army, who had capitulated to the Americans in Italy and been arrested by the French in Austria, safely but illegally over the frontier.

The next day Mr. Ross arrived in a large and elegant Cadillac complete with Austro-Hungarian girl-friend. With her almond eyes and her outlandish appearance she looked a bit dangerous

143

to me, but quite a lot of people did in those days. Irving Ross himself was tall and slim with dark hair and horn-rimmed glasses. He listened to the story, thought it over for a while and then made an extraordinarily simple proposal. As a member of the American secret service he held a diplomatic passport. He proposed to pack me into the boot of his Cadillac and just drive across the frontier into Italy. We tried out the idea on a drive through Innsbruck.

"Get in and draw your legs up," he said. "You ought to be all right. It won't take long."

I did so and he closed the boot behind me. Not only did I have to draw my legs up, but I had to bend my head down and generally adopt a contorted position of the greatest possible discomfort. However suitable the boot of a Cadillac may be for luggage I can inform anybody who happens to be interested that it's lousy as a means of human conveyance. But beggars can't be choosers, and there I was, with the boot cover down behind me and a penetrating smell of petrol and exhaust fumes in my nostrils.

When he started I seemed to bang my head every time we went over a cobblestone and soon I was clinging like grim death to the soles of my worn shoes and trying to make myself shrivel. But at last the trial was over. The car stopped and they opened up the boot.

"Was it all right?" inquired Ross's girl-friend with a sweet smile. I could have slapped her. I felt certain that she had persuaded him to drive over the roughest streets. I just rolled out of the boot and lay for a while outstretched on the ground whilst they all stood round and looked at me like animal trainers teaching a dog a new trick.

However, I was duly grateful to Mr. Ross when he declared three days later that we could now undertake the journey over the Brenner. I crawled back again a little doubtfully into the boot whilst they encouraged me—after all, I already had some experience of that method of travel and they hadn't. But they locked the boot behind me and then got into the car. Captain Bell and his girl friend were going too. They all had passports —and comfortable seats. Ross came round to the back before we started.

"You'll be all right," he said encouragingly. "When we get to the frontier I'll talk so loud that you'll hear everything."

"Then you'll know just what the situation is," added his girl friend.

Then they closed the boot again and climbed in. The engine started up with a roar which made me feel as though I were in a drum with someone banging on the outside, a surge of exhaust gas filled the boot and off we went. It was only ten minutes' drive to the Brenner and everyone except me was in high spirits—we had already drunk quite a lot. They were chattering away in front and gradually the sound of their voices and the hum of the car engine merged into a steady roar in my ears, which felt as though they were going to burst. They didn't burst, but I got a terrible cramp in my legs. I tried to turn over, but it was impossible. In the darkness I could see nothing and I kept banging my head against the steel struts. Soon I could feel blood running down my forehead but I couldn't even raise my hands to wipe it off. It just had to trickle. I began to find it difficult to breathe. My eyes began to smart and my heart to pound. I wanted to beat against the walls of the boot and shout for help, but apart from the fact that I couldn't move my arms the car had now stopped and I could hear the sound of Italian voices. We were on the Brenner. From what I could hear of it they were more interested in the American cigarettes my friends were giving them than they were in passports, for I heard a profusion of lyrical thanks. I could hardly breathe by this time and I wanted to sneeze. Desperately I held my breath. At last the car started up again and drove on. I couldn't have stood even a few more seconds of it.

A few minutes later I was out of that boot and was snowballing with Bell, Ross and their girl friends. After that I sat in the car next to Ross on a long and comfortable seat that stretched across the whole car. I had done it, and already my aches and pains were disappearing.

That evening Ross invited me to dinner in the suite he had taken at a first-class hotel in Bolzano. After the trials and troubles of the day—and many previous days, it was very pleasant to sit there in peace and comfort and drink Mr. Ross's red wine without a care in the world. Whilst we were chatting

Ross spilt some of the wine and it stained the front of his white shirt. It was heavy red wine and immediately it looked to me like blood. My fantasy must have been over-excited by the various events of the recent past and I leant back in my chair and closed my eyes for a moment. But I couldn't get rid of that picture. In fact in my imagination it became even more atrocious—Ross's eyes were gouged out. After a moment or two I recovered, and another drink or two put me right. We parted on the best of terms that evening, looking forward to seeing each other again. We never did. That was the last I saw of Ross.

On November 8th 1948, at a time when I was living like a lord in Lugano, Irving Ross was murdered in Vienna. He had gone there with his girl friend in the same Cadillac in whose boot I had crossed the frontier so uncomfortably and they drove through the Russian sector. Shortly before they came to the South Railway Station the Cadillac was stopped by four men in Russian uniforms armed with sub-machine guns.

Later on the car was found with Ross slumped dead at the wheel. There was blood staining his shirt front and his eyes had been gouged out. He had been bayoneted to death.

CHAPTER VII

SUNNY ITALY AGAIN

I stood in the railway station of Venice; the far-famed city of the Doges, and waited for a young priest, who was to take me to a winter resort. I had stayed in Bolzano for a couple of weeks only, and here I was now in Venice. The whys and the wherefores are not worth going into.

It was a cold January evening in the year 1948. The dirty railway station was swathed in mist, and it was as cold and uninviting as the rest of the town. The sky was overcast and the famous lovers' moon that shines over honeymoon couples on all the travel prospectuses was hardly visible at all. The things that weren't black were grey. The ancient palaces of Venice looked old and dilapidated, which means only that on this particular miserable evening they looked to me for the first time what they really were. The railway station still showed signs of bomb damage, and the force of the explosions had twisted some of its steel girders and left them jutting into the sky like bony arms. I walked up and down to keep myself warm.

From the Canale Grande came a nasty smell of decaying fish. The mist condensed on the roofs and dripped down to the ground in dirty drops. The romantic gondoliers were all in their favourite locals, playing cards. A lonely police launch chugged its way along the canals and the loud popping of its engine died away only after it had disappeared behind the half-ruined walls of ancient warehouses where the riches of former merchant princes had once been stored. One or two railwaymen trudged off to their jobs with tools in one hand and dixies in the other. They all looked rather thin and consumptive in the misty light of the neon tubes. A train was drawn up at the platform and the engine was hissing softly.

The weather was damp and penetrating and I felt cold as I walked up and down examining the few people who were in the station, hoping to spot my priest. In front of the station was a large red neon sign with the one word "Venezia". There was something wrong with the final letter and it kept flickering and going out. Finally it gave up the ghost and only "Venezi" remained, a stump of a word. Somehow it seemed symbolical, but I couldn't think of what. Probably my mind turned to such fruitless exercises because I was chilly and with nothing to do but wait for a priest who hadn't yet turned up. I knew that there was another half an hour to go before the Milan express left to take me together with the priest to the snows of Northern Italy. That was plenty of time for an Italian, but I am a German and my national characteristics give me a thing about train times. I'd much sooner get in half an hour too soon. However, I disciplined myself and stayed on the platform.

I waited there, it occurred to me, as I had waited there ten years before. I had been in civilian clothes then, too. I have always had a habit—which made me suspect with the Nazis— of getting out of uniform on every possible occasion and becoming a civilian again. I don't suppose that in the future I shall have much opportunity of practising it, but in 1938 it was different. On that occasion it had been Balbo's fault. Having met Goering, Balbo expressed a desire to meet Hitler too, so off we went to Berchtesgaden. Once the reception was over my duty as an interpreter was over too and I could be myself again. Whenever I had been compelled to stay more than a few days in the brown atmosphere of the Third Reich I always felt I had earned a holiday out of it. This time I had been there considerably longer and so at the first opportunity I went to Venice.

My uniforms were folded up in my baggage and I was wearing a spotlessly white summer suit. It was midsummer in Venice. I also had on an expensive panama. In this fashionable guise I stood there and waited for my hotel porter, and like my priest so far, he didn't turn up. But then a man came up to me with outstretched hand.

"Ah! You must be Signor Dalman."

Dalman, Dollmann, what was the difference?

"That's right," I said, but I still looked around for someone in uniform who looked as though he might be my hotel porter. But the other man plucked at the arm of my white summer suit.

"Come along, Signor Dalman," he said. "The party is waiting for you."

"What party?" I asked in astonishment.

"Oh, you know, Signor Dalman," he said with a smile and he drew me over to where an old lady with white hair was sitting in an invalid chair. I bowed to her politely. I hadn't the faintest idea who she was, but the stranger was at my side explaining everything.

"This is Mr. Dalman who is going to guide us round Venice," he said to the old lady, and to me he said: "And this is Mrs. Roosevelt, the mother of the United States President."

"Charmed," I said and I bowed again. It was quite clear now that there had been a misunderstanding. Dalman was not a mistake for Dollmann; there must be a Signor Dalman around somewhere. At first I intended to clear up the misunderstanding at once, but the matronly face of the white-haired old lady was looking so pleased at the sight of me and so eager to start doing the sights, that some private little devil urged me to play up to the misunderstanding and show the mother of the United States President round the town of the ancient merchants and shop-keepers of Venice, and I did.

The old lady was pushed along beside me and off we went whilst I expatiated on the civilization of the Occident and the glories of ancient Venice with its Doge palaces and its modern fried-fish parlours, the smell of which, incidentally, made her turn up her nose and doubt the civilization of the present-day Venetians. When we had passed over the Bridge of Sighs and the Americans had fed the pigeons on the Square of St. Mark's with the remains of sandwiches, Mrs. Roosevelt expressed a wish to meet the last of the "Dogaressa". That was Annina Morosini, who was still the uncrowned Queen of the place. Venice now had a mayor and all the usual officials of the twentieth century, but Annina's name and her palace still bore the halo of a lost and more romantic age.

Annina Morosini was already an old woman then, but she had a feeling for the achievements of our modern age, particularly the telephone, and her palace was like an exchange with innumerable black, white and cream telephones. All day long, huddled up in her old-fashioned clothes—only her glowing eyes were to be seen under the black lace headdress—she would sit in the broiling heat and telephone with the rest of the world outside her palace of Renaissance columns. Beside one of these telephones was a yellowing photograph of Wilhelm II, the last German Kaiser.

"A wonderful man!" she exclaimed to me on one occasion. "When he came here he wore a dazzling white uniform with a wonderful steel helmet. Tremendous!"

But just at that moment one of the telephones rang and the lady of the house had to talk at length to a friend about a list of invitations.

Apart from this vast array of telephones, Annina had another foible: a collection of pictures or busts of all the broken-down royalties of Europe together with once great statesmen and financial geniuses. They were all there, a monument to the vanity of human wishes and silent witness to the mutability of all human affairs.

I recalled myself from my memories and looked at my watch. It was two o'clock. My train left at two ten. The last letter of the illuminated station name was still dark and my priest had not turned up. It was raining now, a fine, cold rain which began to soak into my thin coat. Most passengers had already taken their places and the locomotive of the Milan express was beginning to make louder preparatory noises. The only person in sight was an elegantly-dressed young man, but I hardly gave him a second glance: he was obviously not my priest. Even an Italian ought to be thinking about catching the train now, I thought.

The young man came up to me, hat in hand, looking at me a little doubtfully. I took no notice of him and nervously lit a cigarette. The cold wind blew out the match and brought a strong whiff of decaying fish from the lovely lagoons of Venice.

"Excuse me," said the young man, "are you Signor Dollmann?"

I stared at him, astonished that he should know my name. He looked like a fairy, moved like a fairy, and smiled like a fairy. But he turned out not to be a fairy; at least, not primarily a fairy.

"I am," I said. "Who are you?"

150

He smiled, put down his elegant white-leather case, took off his white suede gloves and stroked his white St. Moritz ski outfit.

"I am Don Gabriele Saraceno," he replied. His white teeth glistened and his hair, the colour of black patent leather, shone in the neon light.

"Oh, yes," I acknowledged. "And how is it you know me?"

"I am the private secretary of the Prince Bishop of Görz."

My cigarette nearly fell out of my lips.

"I have come to accompany you to Motta," he went on. "You are informed, I take it?"

"Oh, yes, yes," I said. "Of course, but . . ."

"You mean I don't look like a priest?"

"Yes, that's it. I can hardly credit it."

And I could hardly credit it. His outfit would have suited the son of an American oil magnate on holiday in Saint Moritz —it was beautiful, elegant, and obviously expensive.

"Well, never mind," he said. "Come along. Let's get in."

It was high time and the guard was already blowing his whistle when we got into a first-class compartment. I sat down with relief in the comfortable plush seat and looked out of the window. It was raining harder now. Mist was swirling over the canals. The place still smelt like a fish market after a hot day and the clanking sound of shunting locomotives mingled with the steady beat of our wheels and the chugging sound of a police launch on patrol. Beside me sat the odd priest in his elegant ski costume.

"How does it come about that you haven't the tonsure?" I demanded abruptly.

He smiled sweetly.

"I don't need to," he said.

"Why not, Don Gabriele? You are a priest, aren't you?"

"Oh yes," he said, and from his pocket he produced a packet of imported cigarettes which he opened and offered to me.

"There is a dispensation for the Prince Bishop of Görz, and as his private secretary it applies to me as well."

"And so you don't have to wear a tonsure, or any outward sign that you're a priest?" I went on.

"That is so," he agreed, and he lit himself a cigarette.

151

"That's a very nice ski suit you have on," I said, changing the subject. "I haven't one myself."

"It doesn't matter. That can be arranged."

A pause followed and then for something to say I asked him whether Görz didn't belong to the Free State of Trieste. He agreed that it did.

"You seem to have adapted yourself very thoroughly to the new times, Don Gabriele," I remarked a trifle disagreeably."

"Certainly," he said. "It is very necessary that we should."

Nothing much further was said until we came to Milan where there was a certain liveliness in our coach. Groups of elegant young women in sports dress and with skis got into the train and as they passed our compartment I was astonished to notice that they all greeted Don Gabriele.

"Do you know those young ladies?" I asked.

"Of course I do," he replied, and he bared his teeth in a broad smile. "They are young ladies of the Milan aristocracy and they are going with us to Motta to pray."

"To pray!" I repeated. "They look more as though they were going there for the winter sports."

"That too, of course. Why shouldn't they?"

"Oh, no reason at all. To pray and to ski. Why shouldn't they?"

Early the next morning we were in Motta. It was fresh but not cold and the white snow gleamed in the morning sunlight. Motta is a small mountain village in the Italian Alps not far from the Swiss frontier. It lies over 6,000 feet up above the tree line on a high plateau between enormous mountains and it can be reached only by a narrow mule track.

In the upper village was a long, plain-fronted hotel. A small stone building set there by human hands amidst the mountain giants all around and intended to bring students and other young men nearer to the Church through sport. Lower down in the village was an old peasant house which had been enlarged and extended to serve the same purpose for the girls. Don Gabriele Saraceno led his protégées there.

After long morning prayers Don Gabriele and the young ladies would put on their brand-new ski costumes and go off to their slalom and their ski tours to return once again like obedient school girls with their rather unspiritual protector to the house where a large and romantic fire burned cheerily in a newly-installed fireplace. There they would kneel and squat before the young priest and listen to his tales. There he stood all in white with shining face and black curls and preached to the girls of the Lombardy aristocracy at his feet, telling them stories of female, and of course aristocratic, saints and how they resisted the temptations of the world and the flesh.

And when that was over the young ladies would go to the brand-new kitchen with its cooking utensils of shining enamel and prepare themselves their simple meal of spaghetti with their own virginal hands. And after they had eaten Don Gabriele would lead the daughters of the aristocracy of Upper Italy who had been entrusted to his care up the mule track to the little Chapel of the Madonna in the Snow.

There was a touching story about this chapel. In Motta as in most places there was a prodigal son, and when nothing remained to him but to emigrate to the United States his mother whispered to him with tears in her eyes, "Oh, Carletto, caro Carlette! I will live on until you return, and in storm and rain, mist and snow, the light will always be burning in the window for you." And off he went. After ten years he returned, a rich man. A heavy snow storm did not prevent him from returning to his mother's house, but shortly before he reached it—as in so many such stories—his strength gave out and he sank helplessly into the snow and would have died there. But then the Madonna appeared to him in person, raised him to his feet and led him to the house where his mother awaited him. A last kiss from mother on the forehead of the returned prodigal and the light went out. The patient mother had kept her word and now she died. Whereupon the rich prodigal built the Chapel of the Madonna in the Snow to glorify the miracle.

The young ladies knelt in the chapel under the supervision of Don Gabriele and prayed to the Blessed Virgin, perhaps to thank her for preventing them from falling off the jumping platform whilst ski-ing that day. And at ten o'clock, after a last warm before the flickering fire, they would all go to bed, eagerly discussing the merits of Norwegian wax for their skis.

In the meantime I lived in the alpine home of the young males and was bored to death. I couldn't ski and I was by this time heartily tired of the ever-repeated story of the prodigal son, the miracle in the snow and the founding of the Chapel of the Madonna in the Snow. It was therefore something of a relief to me when one day the handsome Don Gabriele came up to me in the male department and informed me excitedly that a new Night of Saint Bartholomew was at hand.

"A what?" I asked.

"Saint Bartholomew's Night," he repeated. "Elections. Don't you understand?"

"What have elections got to do with Saint Bartholomew's Night?"

"Just that the Communists will be victorious. Yes, it is highly probable that they will be victorious."

"Do you really think so?"

"It's more than probable," he insisted. "It's practically certain. And then there will be a Saint Bartholomew's Night for all the faithful. They will slaughter all priests."

"Do you think they really will?"

"Of course. And you too."

He said this rather sharply, as though he were particularly anxious to make it clear that I was in it as well.

"What, me!" I exclaimed in some surprise.

"Yes. You too. They will kill everyone who belongs to us."

I remembered the Communists of Trastevere who had fed me with spaghetti and plied me with Frascati wine, and then accompanied me home armed with the weapons they had got from the Germans and the Americans.

"The Lord's annointed and all the faithful, all those who are with us. We shall seek protection in the chapel built in the snow in honour of the Blessed Virgin."

"Well, of course I'm one of the faithful," I said, "but personally I think I'd feel safer over the Swiss frontier."

He showed no indignation at my very worldly reaction. He just looked at me calmly, almost casually.

"Yes, that's how it's been planned."

"Planned? Who's planned it?"

Don Gabriele smiled. It was the smile of a martyr, of a man quite certain of being killed for his faith, and resigned to his fate but determined to carry out his last mission before giving up his life.

"To-morrow we shall leave from Milan in a car for the frontier," he said simply.

"But I haven't any proper papers," I objected.

He shook his head contemptuously.

"Papers," he said. "You won't need any papers. Inez will take you over the frontier and nothing will happen to you."

"Who's Inez?" I asked. "I don't know any Inez."

"You will. She was once queen of the Partisans."

"What?" I demanded, and I thought of the elections in which the Communists were to be victorious and of Don Gabriele and the faithful fleeing to the Chapel of the Madonna.

"Queen of the Partisans," he repeated.

"But my dear Don Gabriele, I thought you just said that the Communists were going to slaughter us all after the elections."

"After the elections is after the elections," he replied calmly. "Not now."

"But how can you co-operate with ex-Partisans?"

"Why not?" he asked in surprise. "Or don't you want to be taken over the frontier?"

"Of course I do," I said, and I left it at that. Things were getting too confused: approaching massacres and communist election victories, the flight of the faithful to the Chapel of the Madonna, Partisan queens and the Swiss frontier.

Before long we were on our way in a car to the Swiss frontier. Don Gabriele sat silently beside me and I nervously smoked one cigarette after the other. This wasn't the first time I was crossing a frontier without proper papers, but to be taken over by a former queen of the Partisans through the good offices of a priest was enough to make any man smoke like a chimney.

The car stopped before a little inn not far from Chiasso and we went inside and ordered grappa. It was served in very large glasses. We sipped it as we waited.

"Where's your Partisan Queen, Don Gabriele?" I wanted to know.

He was dressed in an elegant grey suit and he brushed away an imaginary crumb or two.

"Don't bother your head about that, Signor Dollmann," he said with a smile. "She will be here in good time."

There was silence for a while and then he added thoughtfully: "She follows a slightly different profession now."

He said nothing further and once again I was so impressed with the ramifications of the Church and the extent of its influence that I found no comment.

About ten minutes after that Inez arrived. Her name ought to have been Carmen. She had long jet-black hair and golden ear-rings and many bangles on her arms, and round her shoulders was a very colourful shawl. She came up to our table and she looked at me keenly.

"So you want to go over the frontier?" she asked.

I nodded rather uncertainly.

"That's right," I said, "I do."

She laughed and put forward one arm for inspection. There was a long white scar running up it.

"Glancing bullet," she said. "You needn't worry, I've done more difficult things than getting you over the frontier."

I looked at Don Gabriele, but he only smiled and said nothing. After that we finished our grappa and left the inn to pay a visit to the local chapel where we all prayed to the saints for the success of our undertaking, kneeling down together: the former German S.S. Colonel, the private secretary of the Prince Bishop of Görz, and the former Italian Partisan leader. 'It's a pity there isn't a special saint for looking after illegal frontier crossings,' I thought. 'But perhaps St. Christopher will do.'

When we left the chapel Don Gabriele said good-bye.

"Good luck," he called out and he climbed into the big car and was driven away through the snow.

"Well, where do we go from here?" I asked Inez.

She thrust one arm under mine, looked up at me, showing her white teeth in a Carmen smile, and declared to my embarrass-ment: "You're my lover now."

"But . . ." I began to protest.

"Oh, it's all right. Don't get worried. I can see I'm not your type. What I mean is that you must pretend we're lovers."

And with that understanding we made our way towards the Italian frontier post, embracing and kissing and generally behaving like enthusiastic young lovers. At the frontier a customs man was leaning against a level-crossing sort of a gate. He seemed to know my companion well.

"What! a new one, Inez?" he exclaimed.

"Why not?" demanded Inez, and she patted me affectionately. My shirt was sticking to me.

"Having a go at the older generation," the rude fellow commented. I pretended not to have heard. Inez produced a cigarette, let the customs man light it for her, and then she lifted up the gate and drew me through after her.

"What about your papers?" asked the customs man.

She kissed him on the cheek.

"Don't be a fusspot," she said gaily. "We only want to buy a few cigarettes and one or two things on the other side. We'll bring you back something."

The man laughed and pushed her away.

"All right," he said. "Don't be back too late. I'll give you a couple of passes."

He took a block of forms from his pocket, scribbled something on a couple of them and handed them over, then he slapped Inez on the bottom and we went off into No Man's Land.

At the other side we found the Swiss just as friendly, but rather more serious. How they knew the Italian Partisan girl I don't know, but they did, and the same game started up with them, except that out of consideration for the more sober morals of the Confederation Inez behaved herself a little more modestly.

"Where are your papers?" the Swiss controller wanted to know, but Inez opened her eyes wide.

"I've left them at home," she said.

"What about the gentleman? Where are his papers?"

At that Inez cast her eyes down.

"They're in my house too," she murmured.

The Swiss laughed.

"But we only want to go for a walk."

She had her way and the man filled out a couple of temporary passes for us and we strolled into the territory of the Confederation. After we had gone some way we parted.

"You must go on alone now," she said. "No doubt Don Gabriele has given you an address."

I nodded and thanked her warmly for her services, shaking her hand heartily. Then I made my way into Switzerland alone.

CHAPTER VIII

SWISS GÖTTERDAMMERUNG

D
ON GABRIELE had booked me a room in a hotel in Lugano
and there I packed away my few things, took the key
and went out. I sat down beside the lake and ordered a
vermouth. It was not the first time I had sat there; and the
last time it had not been as a passless nobody. Three years
previously, on March 3rd 1945, I had sat on that same terrace
overlooking the lake. I had not been alone. A number of gentlemen of the Swiss General Staff had been there with me, and
instead of vermouth there was a wonderful Swiss breakfast on
the table before me. It was the preliminary stage of the negotiations which had led up to the capitulation.

For the time being there was peace in Europe. The agents
of the American secret service who had come to meet me there
were still around, but they were no longer so visible. New
Italian elections were about to take place, and their upshot was
so feared by Don Gabriele that there I sat once again, but alone
and without a passport in my pocket. I had been right about
the capitulation, but it didn't seem to have done me much good.
However, it was a lovely evening.

I drank three large vermouths and when I finally stood up
I felt a little tipsy and very tired. The next morning I had a
headache and a hang-over. I ordered coffee, and an old Swiss
waiter brought it to my room. I looked suspiciously into the
cup. It contained a liquid which was not easy to identify.

"What's that?" I asked.

"It's coffee, sir," the man replied coolly.

"Coffee, eh? It looks more like vanilla pudding."

"Our guests like it like that with a lot of milk and sugar in it."

I looked at his face and realized that I was being awkward.
I also remembered that I had no passport and had better bob
down.

159

"Very well," I said, "if that's how your guests like it I suppose it will have to do."

The waiter disappeared wordlessly and I quickly drank the contents of the cup. It was too sweet and too oily. Then I washed, dressed and went down into the vestibule to look at the morning papers. "Russians blockade Berlin" said the headlines. "American bombers fly in foodstuffs". What did they care about Berlin here? They had other interests. A large town in North Germany was being blockaded by Russians, and American bombers that had once dropped bombs on it were now dropping bread. Very interesting. But in the meantime I had no passport.

The spring passed and summer arrived to find me still in Lugano, living on I can't remember just what any more. And towards the end of summer my birthday hove in sight. I had bathed and swum, lazed on the promenade and watched the world go by. A lot of things had happened in Europe, but nothing in Lugano. Oh yes, and I had got older of course.

On my birthday I decided to stay longer in bed and skip my usual morning swim, but I was not to be allowed to laze. Jean the waiter knocked at my door.

"Someone wants to speak to you, Signore."

"Who is it?"

The waiter's voice sank to a whisper:

"A very well-dressed gentleman in a car flying a pennant."

That didn't sound like the police, so rather relieved I got up, dressed and went down. I didn't care how well-dressed my visitor was or how many pennants he had flying from his car —as long as he had nothing to do with the police. Unlike the old Europe of kings and princelings, our modern Europe demands that a man shall have a wallet full of identity papers, customs clearances, tax receipts and passports before he is allowed to live peacefully anywhere. And they were precisely the things I lacked. Without them all, a man—be he never so human—is not a complete man.

However, whistling cheerfully, because it was, after all, my birthday, I pushed open the revolving door and there before me was the car: a handsome and expensive Lancia. No, most certainly not the police. And waving on the right mudguard was the flag of the Knights of Malta. My visitor was Baron

Luigi Parrilli, the nobleman who had fetched me from the Villa Fiorita to meet the Americans. Apart from the chauffeur there was also a young and attractive platinum blonde. Parrilli usually travelled accompanied by such adornments and I was never able to discover whether the ladies were atomic spies, nurses or just—companions. Baron Luigi gave me his hand.

"I thought I'd like to look you up, Eugenio. How are you?"

"Thank you," I said, "and how are you?"

The Baron made no reply to that unnecessary question but led me into the adjacent drawing-room as though he owned the place. The platinum blonde followed us silently on crepe-soled shoes. We all sat down and she produced a block and a pencil and recorded every word that fell from the Baron's lips. This recording of everything he said was a habit with him. It was probably some sort of phobia, an exaggerated desire to play safe.

I have forgotten to mention that there was another man with him. His face was vaguely familiar but I couldn't place him. Whilst I was still wondering, Baron Luigi saved me the trouble by introducing him: Signor Lanfranchi, one of the leading journalists of Milan, a man who saw more with his one eye than most other people saw with their two—or would have seen with ten. Baron Luigi clapped his hands and a waiter appeared.

"Champagne," ordered the Baron, and a little later we were sipping excellent bubbly and discussing the complex political situation—that is, after we had spoken of our joint Italian friends.

"Any fantastic plans in view?" I inquired.

Parrilli leaned back in his armchair.

"The poor Germans . . ." he began, but I laughed.

"All right, Eugenio," he said. "I don't want to insult you, but the fact remains that Germany is in a state. There are so many people who haven't any work and haven't enough to eat —and so on."

"And so on," I repeated. "But just what's it got to do with you?"

I could see him looking at me keenly and I had an idea he was up to something. He took another sip of his champagne.

"I am going to Germany as Ambassador Extraordinary and Minister Plenipotentiary of the Sovereign Order of the Knights of Malta."

"Are you now?" I said delightedly. "Wonderful! And what an imposing title!"

He laughed good humouredly.

"Now listen, Eugenio, I thought you would be more interested in my task than my title."

"Not now. Those days are past, my dear Baron. The only interesting things nowadays are titles. Another ominous sign of the times, I suppose."

"You know, Eugenio, when I hear you talk like that I have a feeling that you ought to get out of Europe for a while."

"It's an odd thing, but I get that feeling myself sometimes."

"Good, then perhaps you'd be interested in a leading position in my fleet."

"Your fleet? What's that?"

He took another sip of champagne, made himself comfortable and looked at me.

"Well, as I said, a lot of Germans are very badly off. They'd be glad if someone offered them work and security, so I thought I'd charter a fleet and help them to get to some other part of the world where they'd be better off."

"A sort of Knights of Malta Morgenthau Plan," I said.

Parrilli laughed, but took it in good part.

"You notice everything, Eugenio, but you're much given to exaggeration."

"Where are you thinking of sending them all to?" I asked.

Parrilli studied the bubbling champagne in his glass.

"Patagonia," he said, for all the world as though it were some little village not far from Lugano. "Tierra del Fuego—and round about there."

"You want to shift the Germans to Patagonia!" I exclaimed. It was an extraordinary notion.

"Not all of them," he said drily, "just those who are doing badly in Germany. And there are some very useful people amongst them too."

"And I'm to play a leading role in the business?"

"Yes, if you like. Or don't you like?"

"Is that my share in the re-building of Europe Dulles promised me three years ago in this very place?"

"Why not?" he demanded and turned his attention once again to his champagne.

"So Europe is to be built up in Patagonia? I must say the idea is original."

Parrilli was obviously getting a trifle fed up with my over-critical attitude. He leant forward.

"Will you do me a favour at least?" he asked.

"What then? Take over the supreme command of your emigration fleet?"

He made an irritable movement with his hand. That subject was exhausted. As far as he was concerned the descendants of the ancient Teutons were to go to Patagonia and plant turnips —with or without my co-operation.

"Now you know most of the South-German aristocracy. Give me a few names and addresses, will you?"

The platinum blonde handed me her note-book and I wrote down the names of all the South-German aristocrats I could think of. After all, why shouldn't the Reich's Counts and the Reich's Dukes go to Patagonia and plant turnips together with the unemployed mechanics and carpenters? I didn't mind.

"Do you want to take them all along too?" I inquired, but Parrilli took the list, put it in his pocket book and looked at his watch. Then he stood up and I stood up too. Our little interview it appeared was over. But then he turned to the journalist.

"Oh, by the way, Lanfranchi: didn't we bring along a little birthday present for Eugenio?" he asked.

"We certainly did," replied Lanfranchi, and he began to rummage around in his brief-case. I could see from the half-concealed grin on Parrilli's face that there was to be some surprise, but I didn't expect what I got. Parrilli quickly took something out of Lanfranchi's hand and gave it to me.

My eyes stood out like hat-pegs and I quite lost my voice. It was a new passport of the Italian Republic made out in my name.

"Issued by Police President Polito in person," said Parrilli. "He says that you spoiled his birthday a little while back but he bears no malice."

I had just enough breath left to express my thanks and say good-bye and the little party was in the Lancia and driving off. Parrilli waved and I waved back with my brand-new passport.

The Lancia disappeared and in my hand I held the most important document there is in this modern world of ours: a genuine, valid and authentic passport in my own name. I was a complete man again at last.

With a passport in my pocket my life was changed—psychologically, not outwardly, for I stayed where I was in Lugano and enjoyed myself. The second year dawned and I was still in Lugano, still swimming in the lake in the morning, amusing myself during the day, and sitting by the lakeside in the evening watching the financial and social cream of Europe enjoying itself around me. It was July 1951. My passport still looked like new—I had used it so seldom. But there it was and its mere presence, even unused, gave me a wonderful feeling of security and freedom. It also gave me courage enough to visit Campione.

This little Italian enclave on the free soil of the Confederation contains nothing but a gaming casino maintained by the rich industrialists of Milan. It was the favourite stamping ground of the rich cheese and milk merchants of William Tell's mountains and at the same time a suitable place for the industrialists of Upper Italy to negotiate their international business. Apart from that it was a most convenient spot from which to transfer surplus wealth from Italy into Switzerland, where it escaped the attentions of the tax collector.

It was an interesting place and I found it quite amusing. But one evening I spotted one or two types I knew very well. There was Luigi, for example, and Antonio, and one or two others. They were very neatly dressed, but something about them said "police" a long way off. I went up to Luigi.

"Now listen, Luigi," I said. "No nonsense, please. I've got a proper passport and all my affairs are in order. You can see my passport if you like."

Luigi smiled and looked round cautiously.

"No, no, Signor Dollmann," he replied. "Nothing like that. We are here for another reason."

"Are you sure?" I queried doubtfully.

"Quite sure, Signor Dollman. We are here to protect a king."

"A king, eh?"

There was no time to inquire which king—there weren't many left—for at that moment the swing doors of the hall were flung back and in came a vast clot of a man preceded by the director of the casino almost on his knees, and followed by about ten Pashas and a number of young ladies with liquid eyes. It was His Majesty King Farouk of Egypt, still formally on the throne at that time. The barrel-like monarch of the Nile was dressed in a cream-coloured silk suit which did up the front with a zip fastener and was worn at the moment in deep décolleté out of which a mass of hair curled up proudly. Out of each ear more hair sprouted.

Farouk sat down heavily at the gaming table and then the thousand-franc notes began to fly. Opposite him stood the devout mass of Swiss milk and cheese merchants and humbly watched His Majesty losing thousands. The Italian industrialists, on the other hand, gleefully joined in the game. Farouk ignored them completely. Every now and again he took another dollop of money from a Pasha behind him and proceeded to lose that too. It was an elevating sight.

Signor Bianchi regarded me as amongst the privileged ones of this world, for had I not eaten my "capitulation dinner" with the new masters of the world in his most excellent Ristorante "Biaggi" in Lugano on March 3rd 1945? That historic meal had of course not taken place in the public restaurant frequented by the well-to-do citizens of Lugano on the ground floor, but in the sacrosanct meeting place of the local Lugano Rotary Club on the first floor, well away from all prying eyes. The restaurant itself looked something like the interior of a particularly revolting Florentine chapel of the nineties, but fortunately the wines and the food that Signor Bianchi served there would have been more at home in the Renaissance. The same could not be said of his guests. "Late Baroque" would have suited most of them better.

But perhaps the reader is wondering how it came about that just over three years previously, whilst the war was still raging, I should have been honoured in such a fashion—and who had done the honouring?

The moving spirit was my old friend Parrilli, a cheerful but cunning gentleman to whom I have already referred. At the beginning of 1945 he had used the good offices of his old friend

Professor Max Husmann in Lugano to get into touch with the innocently named American Office of Strategic Services, or, in other words, the American Secret Service, and with its European chief Mr. Allen W. Dulles, the special representative of President Roosevelt in Europe. Baron Parrilli had been determined for some time to move heaven and earth if need be to save Upper Italy from destruction and to prevent the retreating German forces from applying a policy of "scorched earth", which would have meant the ruin of Italy's industrial installations there. As an Italian, of course, Parrilli was a patriot, but in this case his patriotism was reinforced by his personal interests. Chiefly thanks to his enormously rich father-in-law, the big Milan industrialist Posch, Baron Parrilli was also a captain of industry with a big stake in the fate of industry in the North Italian plain.

As a suitable instrument for his plans he chose me. Perhaps that was because I knew as much about industry as he knew about the Dialogues of Plato, but it was probably also because he knew very well about my rather adolescent and foolish passion for Italy, which I had probably sucked in with my mother's milk.

His other friend, Professor Husmann, was originally a Pole but now he was a free citizen of the Confederation and head of the fashionable boys' school at Montana am Zugerberg. In addition, his relationship with Mr. Dulles was excellent.

At the end of February Parrilli returned from a visit to Switzerland with the information that the O.S.S. would be willing to engage in non-committal discussions with me in Lugano concerning the important problems the situation in Italy now raised. General Wolff, who was the first to hear the tidings, called me to his headquarters in Fasano, and there we discussed the sensational proposal at some length. Germany had lost the war; that was quite clear for both Wolff and me. Further, for the moment at least there was no hope of driving a wedge between East and West. And in this situation our only card of any value was the still unbroken front of Field Marshal Kesselring in Italy.

As a result of our discussion therefore I crossed the border at Chiasso as arranged and was lovingly received by Baron Parrilli, who was accompanied by two other civilians: Professor Max

Husmann and a younger man who was subsequently introduced as Lieutenant Rothpletz of the Swiss intelligence service.

As a professional pedagogue it was clearly Husmann's job to put me through my paces and, apparently on the assumption that I was a professional soldier and that my historical knowledge would hardly go much beyond the discovery of gunpowder, he delivered a polite but condescending lecture in which Napoleon's exile on St. Helena played the role of horrible example. I listened equally politely, making a non-committal comment from time to time, and the car in which we were now travelling rolled over the Melida Bridge towards Lugano.

I don't know what marks I got but they were obviously high enough to open the exclusive doors of the Lugano Rotary Club to admit me, and there Husmann's great moment came. He delivered a long lecture on the hopeless situation of Germany for my benefit, concluding. with the solemn assurance that the Western Democracies were the loyal and devoted brothers in arms of Eastern Communism. Still further, it even appeared that arm in arm and shoulder to shoulder the President of the United States and the new Generalissimo of Bolshevist Russia were about to open up a new era in human history.

After that came the nigger in the woodpile: the capitulation of the German and Italian armies in Italy would greatly facilitate the establishment of this new world. So far I had heard nothing about Churchill and Great Britain in all this and my modest inquiry as to whether they were in it too provoked no enthusiasm. I was just fobbed off with the general observation that there would be room for everyone in the new world.

And what about Germany? The professor was ready for that too: only surrender, unconditional surrender, could save Germany now. At that I inquired how the Herr Professor thought Field Marshal Kesselring and General Wolff would feel if I went back and presented them with that as the result of our friendly negotiations. I pointed out that they had both shown a great deal of understanding for the material and human problems of the Italians in the territory they occupied, but that Field Marshal Kesselring was still the commander of an intact and undefeated army of something like a million men. Might he not feel that there was a danger that the words "unconditional surrender" might well be regarded as identical with "betrayal" by some people?

The word "betrayal" set the professor off on a monologue that may have made Cicero turn in his grave. The professor's *De Tradimento* was a piece of dialectical pyrotechnics which embraced just everything and culminated in the solemn assurance that the unconditional surrender proposed would save whatever was still to be saved and by that very token logically excluded even the mere suggestion of betrayal. Then he added cautiously that, of course, concessions in the sense of honourable terms and prompt demobilization of the Italian army on Italian soil would be positively and constructively considered. At this the professor was off again, but Baron Parrilli was bored to tears by this time and to give himself something to be interested in he proposed a pause for lunch.

I don't know whether I was supposed to play the role of repentant sinner in sackcloth and ashes, but in any case I did nothing of the sort. I enjoyed that lunch hugely—and a very good lunch it was—and at the same time I kept my hosts constantly attentive with a never-ending series of stories of former dinners and luncheons in Roman society, interspersed with interesting private experiences from my career as confidential interpreter to the great ones of the Axis Powers. To my secret delight I could see that the whole situation was upsetting the professor and making him more and more nervous and restless.

But my important opposite number, the representative of Mr. Dulles, had not arrived from Berne, and as nothing further could be done without him the party broke up to meet again later. I found the spring on Lake Lugano very attractive so I plunged into it on my own. For one thing I had noticed the bookshop windows on the way, full of rare international titbits. I bought Bromfield's *Miss Parkington, Churchill's War Speeches* and several pounds worth of illustrated British, American and other magazines, and loaded in this way I returned to the premises of the Rotary Club where I found that in the meantime the personal representative of Mr. Dulles had arrived in the shape of Mr. Paul Bloom.

We greeted each other politely but formally and the discussions began. What he had to say was clear and to the point:

Germany had lost the war; neither Hitler nor Himmler was to play any role in the capitulation negotiations as far as the Italian front was concerned; officially and formally the capitulation would have to be unconditional, but that did not exclude the possibility of honourable special terms and personal facilities arrived at by a gentleman's agreement. In conclusion Monsieur Bloom even found a hopeful word or two for the German parties to the capitulation negotiations and their future prospects: *Les destructions materiélles et morales en Europe á cause de cette guerre sont si gigantesques que les Alliés ont besoin de chaque homme de bonne volonté pour la reconstruction. Toutes les personnes qui aident á abreger la guerre donnent preuve de leur bonne volonté.*

No mean prophetic gift would have been necessary to divine behind these fine words concerning our co-operation in the re-construction of Europe the treatment that actually awaited us. I have already done something in the previous pages to describe the quaint American interpretation of our co-operation which subsequently came into operation, and I have no doubt that if put to it General Wolff could contribute further illuminating material from his Nuremberg days, including the time they put him in a lunatic asylum. And then of course there was the death sentence passed on Kesselring, though afterwards commuted. In retrospect it all looks a bit odd, but never mind. Martyrs are always boring, particularly when they really ask for it by their credulity and trustfulness.

In the meantime I sat back and let myself be borne along on the waves of Monsieur Paul Bloom's eloquence to a future of co-operation in the building up of our dear old Europe under entirely new management. Having cast the bait M. Bloom was no doubt inwardly amusing himself hugely at the silly Boche who was swallowing it hook, line and sinker.

At the end of this odd meeting at the Lugano Rotary Club M. Bloom handed me a slip of paper—it reminded me of a game of forfeits at a schoolgirls' party. On it were two names: Parri and Usmiani. Baron Parrilli then explained to me that Mr. Dulles personally attached great importance to the immediate freeing of these two leaders of the Italian Resistance who had been arrested by us, and that if we handed the two men safely over to the Allies he would regard it as an earnest of the *bonne volonté* previously referred to.

I listened with no enthusiasm. That was going to be awkward, particularly on account of "General" Feruccio Parri, the vice-commandant of the North-Italian Partisan Detachments. However I promised to do my best. It was in fact very awkward, but in the end I was successful despite considerable opposition, and a few days later the two heroes were safely over the Swiss frontier and on March 8th Mr. Dulles was able to visit his protégé in Zurich, where, with tears in his eyes, Parri declared that General Wolff's action had been most humane and that he would never forget it as long as he lived. Signor Parri proved to have been over optimistic about the length of his memory. However, before long the Italian people were presented with their first post-war Minister-President in the person of "General" Parri, and I have since heard from a number of his fellow countrymen that the Italians resented our action more bitterly than anything else that was done to them throughout the Second World War.

We all parted in great good humour: M. Bloom because the reconstruction of Europe was now a big step nearer, Baron Parrilli because there was now every hope that the earth of Northern Italy would escape scorching, the professor because I had passed my exam, Lieutenant Rothpletz because he had succeeded in slipping in a good many references to William Tell, and I because I had enjoyed my little jaunt into the spring of Lugano. There were handshakes all round and an almost happy leavetaking.

The next day I reported back to General Wolff, giving him the complete truth without frills and presenting both the bad and the good sides of the conference at the Rotary Club. No door had been closed and a number had now been opened. As far as we were concerned all that remained was to take the sting as far as possible out of the phrase "unconditional surrender" —it had already proved fatal to many of our fellow countrymen who had been arrested after July 20th. We hoped by means of further discussions and verbal agreements to secure honourable terms which would leave open possibilities of future development. In particular I advised Wolff, in the interests of an understanding, to send Parri and Usmiani to their patron Mr. Dulles as requested. Mussolini, who still existed as a weary shadow of his former self, would of course be furious, but what did that matter? The mumbling roars of a toothless old lion mustn't be allowed to compromise something of real importance. The German Security Service in Italy wouldn't like it either. Parri had been a very valuable prisoner in their hands. But after all the trouble the gentlemen of the Security Service had caused, we felt that it was about time that they showed themselves a little more helpful.

And finally I strongly recommended General Wolff as "The Supreme S.S. Commander and Police Chief in Italy" to go to Switzerland at once to get into direct touch with the Americans as they requested. And this he did a few days later.

And now, once again in Lugano, and once again in the Ristorante Biaggi I sat at a table and waited for Signor Bianchi to come over to me and discuss my lunch, as he usually did, but at the moment, as I observed, he was engaged in a discussion with a rather over-dressed young gentleman at the bar. It seemed to be something important, for Bianchi was gesticulating vigorously. In the end, to my surprise, both of them came over to my table.

"This young gentleman wishes to speak to you, Signor Dollmann," said Bianchi.

And I noticed that as well as carefully-pomaded hair the young man also had polished finger nails. Bianchi then withdrew discreetly and the young man bowed and introduced himself.

"Giorgio Rossi," he said and he drew a silver cigarette case from his pocket, opened it and offered me a cigarette. I could see that they were one of the most expensive brands to be obtained in Switzerland. Somehow or other the young gentleman in the sky-blue corduroy jacket didn't look as though they were his usual smoke. However, I took one and he sat down at my invitation.

"Are you just going to have your lunch?" he inquired.

"I was," I said, "but it can wait. And what is it you want of me?"

171

He pretended that he hadn't heard the question, leant back in his chair and let his dark eyes travel round the restaurant.

"Wonderful here in Switzerland, isn't it?"

The tone of his voice almost made me say that I found it all horrible, but he went on:

"Wonderful hotels, silver mirrors, golden chairs . . . and so on."

"Not gold," I said, wondering what all this enthusiasm about the elegance of Switzerland was leading to. He looked at me, and seemed to grow serious, as though he were about to come to the real point.

"No, not real gold of course."

He puffed out a cloud of smoke and then he said suddenly:

"I am here at the instructions of Jim and Joe, Mr. Dollmann."

That gave me a bit of a shock.

"Oh," I said. "Well, what is it you want?"

"I want to ask you something."

"Any missions?"

"Something of the sort," he replied and stubbed out his cigarette.

I got up, and he looked at me in a rather startled fashion, something like a youth who suddenly realizes that he can't do what he has been told to do because he's too dumb.

"I have made a habit of going to church to get away from missions," I said.

"It isn't really a mission," he admitted.

"Isn't it? Nevertheless I'll go to church first. Come with me."

He hesitated a moment and then he stammered:

"But we'll be coming back here?"

"What for? We can just as well go to my place."

"Your place? Where do you live then?"

"If you come from Jim and Joe you ought to know that."

He considered the matter for a moment.

"Naturally," he said, "but I've ordered a meal here."

"In that case," I said indifferently, "there's no reason why we shouldn't come back."

I went out of the restaurant and he followed me to the Cathedral, walking behind me without saying a word. He seemed to be thinking things over, like a schoolboy having difficulties with his homework. I went through the great door of the Cathedral into the cool nave and in the yellow light I really examined his clothes for the first time. He was wearing light half-leather shoes with thick crepe rubber soles and rather short trousers which revealed silk socks with rings in various colours. His trousers looked as though they had been pressed only a little while before, and in addition to his light-blue corduroy jacket he had a silk tie.

When I genuflected before the high altar I noticed that Rossi remained standing with his hands behind his back pretending to study the roof. He had also not taken holy water from the stoup as he came in. Why? He said he was an Italian, but he didn't bow to the high altar and he didn't take holy water and make the sign of the cross. He said he came from Jim and Joe, but he had done himself up like an organ-grinder's monkey.

We went back to the restaurant as arranged and we were served with a copious meal which he had ordered but not chosen. At that he started his praise of Switzerland again.

"Wonderful, isn't it?" he said. "The Swiss food."

"Is this the first time you have been in Switzerland?" I inquired.

"Oh yes," he said cheerfully. "The first time."

"That's odd, isn't it? I thought you were with the American Secret Service."

"Of course, of course," he said but he flushed and lowered his face over his plate. Little more was said until the end of the meal. Then he poured me out another glass of wine.

"Shall we get down to business now?" he asked.

"Why not?" I returned.

He leant his pomaded head over the table towards me and said expectantly,

"Jim and Joe would like to know your opinion of Kesselring."

"Would they really?" I said, and I knew that the question could not possibly come from them, for both of them were excellently informed both about me and Kesselring. I was wondering where the devil he had come from when I heard him say sharply:

"Well, Mr. Dollmann?"

"That's an odd sort of tone to adopt," I said.

"I beg your pardon," he replied and he turned on his sweetish smile again. "I didn't intend it."

"Very well then," and acting on a sudden impulse I declared: "I think Kesselring is the greatest living general."

Rossi's eyes sparkled eagerly.

"Really? You think he's the greatest living general."

"Undoubtedly," I returned. "The man's a genius."

"A genius, eh? And what about Churchill?"

"Oh, he's a genius too."

I had already determined to describe everyone he mentioned as a genius. The effect was exhilarating. Rossi immediately ordered another bottle of wine. In his excitement he spilled some of it on the cloth as he filled up my glass. The red stain it left on the tablecloth spread. And suddenly I realized what stable this absurd person came from with his would-be elegance, his ringed socks, his sky-blue jacket, his naïve astonishment about the marvels of life in Switzerland, and, above all, his unintelligent questions. He could only be a Communist, and I began to laugh.

"What are you laughing at?" he asked with sudden suspicion.

"The state of the world," I said, and I emptied my glass and pushed it over to him for some more of the wine his Party was paying for. "Everything is so absurdly complicated."

"That's just what Jim and Joe say," he said, nodding his head in vigorous approval. "That's just why they want to know what you think about the world situation."

"Just tell them . . ." And my face grew serious and I adopted a solemn tone of voice. ". . . that the world situation depends on the social and economic conditions prevailing in the individual countries."

"Of course," exclaimed Rossi enthusiastically. That was the sort of talk he had heard in his Party lectures. "How true!"

"But . . ." And I looked at him sternly. ". . . you mustn't tell Jim and Joe that. As patriotic Americans they can't accept that at all."

I did my best not to laugh. It was obvious that for the moment he had forgotten in whose service he was supposed to be here.

174

"No, naturally they can't," he agreed. "They shot your dog, didn't they. Can you ever forgive them for that?"

"Never," I said with determination. "Never."

It tickled me to see the way this naïve youth was letting his communist slip show.

"And then these imperial . . ." He almost bit his tongue off. He had just remembered that he was supposed to be in the service of these same imperialists and that his ringed silk socks and his sky-blue corduroy jacket were supposed to create an impression of real Americanism. He now did his best to look like an American Secret Service man.

"Wait a minute," I said. "I want to make a phone call."

"But Jim and Joe . . ." he began anxiously. He didn't want me to go and he didn't want me to make a phone call.

"That's all right," I said soothingly. "They won't mind. They'll be very satisfied with you. I'll be back in a minute."

He looked at me in relief and sank back again in his seat. In the telephone booth I was able to laugh to my heart's content. Then I rang up a couple of my best friends.

"Listen," I implored. "Come over to Bianchi's at once. I've got a Communist agent here. The most wonderful example you ever did see. He's pretending to interview me on behalf of the American Secret Service."

They were there in about ten minutes. In the meantime Giorgio had drunk a good deal more of the strong Swiss wine and he was far more happy than his Party programme would ever have allowed.

"We're going now," I said, and we took him outside and put him into a car.

"Where are we going?" he asked doubtfully.

"Back to my place," I answered, "but first of all to another local where you can see for yourself how many spies and agents there are walking around in Switzerland."

"Excellent," he muttered. Then he sat up. "There aren't any Communist spies there, are there?"

"Heaps of them," I assured him, "but as a member of the American Secret Service, you'll certainly know them all."

"Of course, of course," he said, and he sank gratefully back into his seat.

We obtained a table in one corner of the room near the window. After a few more glasses of wine Giorgio became livelier than ever. Eagerly he stared at the couples dancing in the centre of the floor and then when the band began a boogie-woogie he sprang up, rushed over to a near-by table and carried off a rather surprised young lady of good family who was too well-bred to protest. It was a sight for the gods: there was the agent of the Communist Party, dancing a decadent boogie-woogie in a luxury haunt of imperialists with a member of the upper classes and thoroughly enjoying himself, obviously quite forgetting his role.

Late that evening we took him to the railway station. He was thoroughly drunk by this time.

"It was wonderful," he insisted. "Wonderful."

I patted him on the shoulder in farewell.

"After the feast comes the reckoning," I said. "The Little Father and his boys are going to be very angry with you."

The thing had been a joke and we had all laughed heartily over it, but nevertheless when I began to think over its implications seriously I concluded that it would be better for my health if I went to Zürich for a while and I did. The contented atmosphere of capitalist Zürich with its chocolate and its cakes with cream would suit me quite well for the time being.

It was odd, but hardly had I left the train in Zürich to enjoy the paradise of all German-Swiss, the Bahnhof Strasse, when I had a sudden attack of what I call my memory trouble. It seems to be some sort of outwardly induced schizophrenia with frequent lucid intervals. For example, when I see a church I immediately recall all the princes of the church with whom I have ever had anything to do; the sight of a general produces a long line of generals out of the past; a flat-footed civilian conjures up the host of secret-service men who have honoured me with their attentions. And since the end of the war the appearance of a G.I. immediately unrolls a panorama of all I owe to the great republic across the seas. The attacks vary in length; sometimes I am compelled to follow the line of development they open up for hours on end, reconstructing the whole history of what they meant to me.

And I suffered just such an attack as soon as I got into the

Bahnhof Strasse. It started when I looked into the glittering showcases of the jeweller Meister but caught sight of a middle-aged gentleman standing beside me who was looking at them too. He was obviously comfortably off and his slightly plumpish features suggested long years of good eating and drinking. He might have owned a leather business in Lodz or a chocolate factory in Switzerland. On the other hand he might have had some discreet connection with high politics. A good cigar in the corner of his mouth confirmed the original appearance of well-being, and in addition he was rather too carefully well dressed and on his head was a black Borsalino with a broad band.

And then suddenly I remembered: politics! That was it. It was none other than my old history master Professor Max Husmann. He turned away and under the influence of my obsessional schizophrenia I followed him. And, yes, as I thought, he led me to the Sonnegstrasse, number 80, a typical Swiss urban villa that might have been built to suit the taste of Wilhelm II. He disappeared into the rather pompously-oppressive hall and in spirit I followed him as General Wolff and I had followed him in reality on March 3rd 1945.

That was just five days after my little trip into the Lugano spring I have already described. General Wolff had taken my advice and set off for Lugano as quickly as possible to make direct contact with the Americans and carry on from where I had left off. Everything had gone swimmingly. On the frontier at Chiasso we had once again been met by the same team: Parrilli, Husmann and Rothpletz. But this time it was Wolff who was put through his intellectual paces by the worthy professor. This was in the train on our way to Zürich. The professor had forgotten nothing. No doubt acting on behalf of Mr. Dulles, he introduced Hitler, Roosevelt, Churchill and Dulles himself, the question of obedience and independent thought, lawful orders and individual conscience, and all the rest of it. But the conclusion was the same as before: in principle the capitulation would have to be unconditional; however that did not exclude the possibility of verbal agreements for a rather more generous and elastic arrangement whose fulfilment could be guaranteed by Swiss and Italian personalities: Husmann and

177

Parrilli, and a prominent Swiss whose name should be as yet unmentioned.

By the end of all this we were in Zürich: two high S.S. officers in the company of Swiss civilians and under the protection of President Roosevelt's personal representative in Europe, Mr. Allen W. Dulles. For the benefit of outsiders we were members of a commission to discuss matters relating to the harbour of Genoa, in which the Swiss were deeply interested for import and export reasons.

Following Professor Max Husmann into his Zürich home we were welcomed by a small and rather undistinguished-looking civilian with glasses who preferred to remain anonymous but who subsequently turned out to be Dr. Max Waibel, a Major on the Swiss General Staff, Intelligence Department. There we had another excellent lunch, which greatly improved the general spirits as good lunches usually do. After that, following on a number of mysterious telephone conversations conducted by our host, we were taken off in a car to meet the important Mr. Dulles himself. On the way Wolff was asked:

"Are you here at the instance of Himmler, or on your own initiative following on the contact between Parrilli and Dollmann?"

To which Wolff replied shortly: "Himmler knows nothing at all about it."

The question was one more indication of the distrust our capitulation partners felt towards us, though the initiative was ours and not Himmler's and even against Himmler.

After a polite reception at the hands of Dulles, Max Husmann took the floor again and put the situation more or less as he had put it to me in Lugano: Germany had lost the war; the negotiations between us must be confined to the Italian theatre of war; the capitulation must be unconditional; and finally— once again!—the indissoluble alliance between East and West, between the Anglo-Saxons and the Russian Bolshevists.

Wolff's discussion with Dulles himself, who had received his visitor in the presence of his secretary Gero von Gävernitz, a German emigrant, was at first cool, though very correct, but after a while it became more human and understanding. In the meantime Parri and Usmiani had been freed, as Dulles had requested, and this and the information about the art treasures that had been rescued from the Uffizi and Pitti palaces, and the safe-keeping of the priceless numismatic collection of King Victor Emmanuel, did something to improve the atmosphere. Dulles had obviously been filled with naïve astonishment to hear that the S.S. leadership—of all the unlikely people from his point of view—had removed six hundred paintings and fifty sculptures, all great works of art, from the neighbourhood of Florence, where they had been stored, to the north to save them from possible destruction during Allied bombardments.

With this a bridge had been built and the capitulation discussions proper proceeded in a more conciliatory form. Dulles certainly insisted that the fateful expression "unconditional surrender" must be accepted formally, but he added too that this did not exclude the possibility of unofficial accommodations.

It was evening when Wolff returned and Zürich was brilliantly lit up. However it had been decided that for security reasons we should enjoy the lights only from the balcony, and the professor's wife had in the meantime prepared sleeping accommodation for us. Only friend Parrilli ventured out into the adventurous night life of the most puritanical town in Europe, but even he was back by midnight—with a bottle or two of champagne.

The following morning we were taken by car to a further discussion in the Berner Strasse, where the Swiss office of Mr. Dulles was situated. There we were welcomed by the handsome Gero von Gävernitz, the right-hand man of the chief of the O.S.S. His Jewish mother had no doubt given him those beautiful black curls and she had probably had quite a lot to do with his decision to turn his back on his Fatherland and emigrate to the New World. I already knew him from a fireside chat in the winter of 1940 in the house of a joint acquaintance in Rome. Looking back on it now I can see that that evening might have been a valuable and illuminating one for me, and that it had probably been arranged intentionally, but at that time I was so taken up with the role I was playing in Rome and my supposed social successes that I didn't catch on.

The gentleman who stood before us now was very much the calm and collected victor. Gisevius notes in his book that von

Gävernitz "was astoundingly well informed about German affairs", but really there was nothing surprising about that: the man was a German, and the questions he put and the formulations he used were further proof of it. The interview added nothing new to what had already been said. Everything was recapitulated, supplemented where necessary, and clarified.

After that Wolff and I drove straight to the station and took the Gotthard express to the sunny South; in the company of Dr. Waibel this time. On the way we played a little game to while away the time, a sort of excursion into Cabinet building. The following list which emerged from it may serve as an indication of our naïvete, credulity and confidence in our negotiating partners:

Reich's President: Field Marshal Albert Kesselring; Foreign Minister: well, who better than von Neurath, who had already done the job once and knew his way about? Finance Minister? That was very simple: Papa Schacht, of course, the man who had held down the job—or so it began to seem—from the days of Hermann the Cherusker to Adolf Hitler. And as Minister of the Interior, General Wolff himself seemed as good as any, though Professor Husmann had suggested a special portfolio as re-educator of the German youth for him.

But man proposes . . . A few months later all our ministers and collaborators were safely tucked away in the cells at Nuremberg or in the various Allied war-criminal camps in Germany and Italy. And none of them took any part in the process of reconstruction so solemnly conjured up for us all by Monsieur Bloom.

However, a cold wind began to blow on our little idyll as soon as we crossed the frontier. Two items of bad news were waiting for us: Field Marshal Kesselring had left Italy to relieve Rundstedt as Commander-in-Chief in the West, and the Chief of the Reich's Security Office in Berlin, Kaltenbrunner, urgently wanted to see Wolff.

If I were now to describe all the ups and downs, the fortunes and misfortunes of the capitulation process, I should need another book to do it in. On March 19th there was another meeting in Ascona, where, in addition to Parrilli, Husmann and von Gävernitz there were two Allied generals, an Englishman named Airey and an American named Lemnitzer, who were waiting for Wolff to get the capitulation going. It was at this meeting that Mr. Dulles gave us our good-conduct marks:

"President Roosevelt says he is delighted at the fact that for the first time any German personality has negotiated concerning the possibility of peace, or surrender, without putting forward any personal or material demands on his own behalf. The President is happy to think that contact has now been established with such a group. Negotiations had been opened up previously with various diplomats, officials, officers and industrialists, as I have good cause to know, because I was shaken at the time to discover the selfish personal motives that lay behind them."

Mr. Dulles then turned to Wolff and continued:

"Although you have put forward no demands of a personal nature whatever, and although you have not even asked for any undertaking concerning your future activities in Germany, I hope nevertheless that after the surrender has been carried through we shall be able to count on your co-operation and that of your closest associates."

Wasn't that nice now? Such manly, upright and heartening words from President Roosevelt and his special representative in Europe, Mr. Allen W. Dulles! I even felt that the bit about "your closest associates" included me. But the future was to turn out rather different.

With the sudden transfer of Kesselring we had lost a personal friend, a selfless adviser, and our most important source of strength in the coming negotiations. It is true that from the beginning he regarded the capitulation negotiations purely from the military point of view, but nevertheless it was always possible to speak with absolute frankness to the man who was in supreme command of Germany's forces in Italy. With his departure things were very different.

And now the miniature Heydrich in Berlin, Ernst Kaltenbrunner, the chief of the Reich's Security Office, was apparently taking a hand in the game. The sword of Damocles was suspended over our heads. It meant a series of journeys to Berlin for Wolff, who had to defend himself, his family and what he stood for. And he never knew each time whether he would emerge safely from the lions' den. First of all there was an interview on March 24th with Himmler, who was in disfavour with the Führer and who in his vacillation and uncertainty didn't know what to do next. All he could hope for was that the Western and Eastern Allies would fall out.

In the meantime Kaltenbrunner was intriguing against us, and his only aim seemed to be to save himself and get his past overlooked by arranging a capitulation on his own. There were no further pleasant journeys to Switzerland for me and the moves for the capitulation threatened to go under in complete chaos. In particular, Kesselring's successor, General von Vietinghoff, proved to be a difficult and indecisive character. He was unable to make up his mind, and the Allies were now growing more and more impatient and doubtful of the whole business. On April 18th the next move from Berlin was an order for General Wolff to appear before Hitler himself.

On two occasions Wolff went to the famous bunker of the Reich's Chancellery for interviews with Hitler himself, and on each occasion the whole plan hung by a hair. On the second occasion the man whose trembling hands still held the fate of the German people answered Wolff's question as to whether Germany had definitely decided to come to terms with the West exclusively. Only a shadow of his former self and artificially kept going by injections and drugs, Hitler exclaimed:

"By no means! I shall ally myself with whichever of the two unnatural partners offers me the best conditions for continuing the struggle against the other. Or, in the alternative, with whichever of them first gets into touch with me."

But at least Wolff returned to Lake Garda with his head still on his shoulders and with a vague sort of permission to maintain the contact he had established with the Americans.

The last act of the drama was now approaching. Whilst Wolff with the two officers who were to sign the capitulation at the Allied Headquarters in Caserta, went off to Switzerland I went to Munich to inform Field Marshal Kesselring "discreetly" how far things had gone. On April 26th I was once again in the presence of the man for whom I had always felt an unusual emotion: respect. On the long journey along the Brenner Road, at that time very much harassed by low-flying fighter planes strafing anything they could find, I thought of the Field Marshal I was going to meet and whom I had met on dozens of occasions previously, and once again it was borne in on me how fundamentally unlike the type of political soldier the days of the Weimar Republic had produced in Germany Kesselring really was. And yet it was never impossible to talk politics with him. Kesselring was a non-political soldier but he had a very sound grasp of political affairs, and during the period I was seconded to him he had always been my sheet anchor amidst my numerous difficulties from Rome to Lake Garda.

When I met Kesselring again on April 26th 1945 at Pullach near Munich he had lost nothing of his charm and considerateness, but many things had changed. For one thing, his old bitterness at the excesses of the highest Nazi clique was now replaced by a weary sarcasm. And for those who knew him it was fairly clear that although Kesselring the soldier might still feel himself bound by his oath to Hitler, Kesselring the man did not.

I had come to inform him of the developments which had taken place since his transfer and to give him a politically clear picture of the situation in the Italian theatre of war, to tell him about Wolff's last journey to Berlin and to let him know that everything in the South now demanded a clear and speedy decision. I mentioned Wolff's journey to Switzerland with the two other officers, but without going too deeply into the last-minute details of which in any case I had no very clear picture myself.

"What will you do, sir," I asked. "What answer will you give to the German people if at the critical moment they should appeal to your sense of responsibility?"

"You can be sure that in such a situation I would not hesitate to place everything I have and am at their disposal," he replied.

That was enough. I wanted no more for the moment. On the whole I could assume that Kesselring knew a great deal and that he guessed still more. Perhaps, too, he was glad not to have to take any final decision at the moment.

I took another look at the lighted windows in the Sonneg Strasse. Behind them was the professor with his fat cigar between his rather thick lips. From every point of view he had done very well indeed out of our surrender I had heard. The thought of so much smug satiety displeased me and I decided to turn for refreshment to Mother Nature. Poetic Swiss friends of mine had assured me that at sundown the swans on the lake of Zürich sang their legendary song. A swan song? That would just suit me at the moment, so there I turned my steps.

In April 1945 the same sort of melody was the background to our capitulation efforts. Wolff and the others went off to Lucerne, where Allied representatives were patiently waiting for them—only to learn that the whole proposal was now seriously endangered owing to Russian objections. But at least they had obtained from Major Waibel—who had at last consented to abandon his anonymity—the happy assurance that although there could be nothing in writing concerning honourable conditions of surrender and favoured treatment for the German Army in Italy we could safely rely on the integrity of the Allies, and that further, he, Dr. Waibel, as a Major of the Swiss General Staff, would give his word of honour as a soldier that the guarantees undertaken by him would be fulfilled. From Winkelried to William Tell and Major Waibel—a Swiss man, a Swiss word! And so we accepted hopefully. Apparently Professor Max Husmann had not taken us far enough in our history lessons.

On April 29th the two delegates of Wolff and von Vietinghoff, who had at last made up his mind, signed the capitulation at Allied Headquarters in Caserta. Its terms were to come into operation at two o'clock in the afternoon of May 2nd—that is to say, if everything went according to plan its terms would come into operation. ... But at the last moment Vietinghoff was transferred and replaced by a General who seemed determined to resist the capitulation to the bitter end. In consequence there was a dramatic scene in Bolzano, where Wolff and the Army Group now had their Headquarters. It was probably unique in the history of the German Army.

In Caserta Field Marshal Alexander was pressing urgently for confirmation that the following afternoon at two o'clock the surrender would actually take place, and in the meantime from the front—if such a thing could still be regarded as existing—came one dismal message after the other. To cut a long story short, the defeated German Army was rolling back without artillery and without munitions and in complete disorder. From Trieste came the glad tidings that the previous day the partisans of Tito had entered the town at a time when the advanced elements of the 8th British Army were still twenty-four hours away. If Tito—with the main Russian forces on his heels—succeeded in forcing the 7,000-man-strong German garrison to surrender with all its weapons and material before the capitulation to the British could take place, then to the east of Trieste across Venice the way into the northern plains would be open and the proclamation of a Soviet republic in Northern Italy would be a matter of days only.

On May 1st in the morning the new commander-in-chief, General Schultz, and his Chief of Staff had been placed under temporary arrest, to be released during the course of the day. At six o'clock in the evening all the commanders of the German forces in Italy were gathered in the rock bunker which was now the German Headquarters, including General Herr of the Tenth Army and General Lemmelsen of the Fourteenth Army. In addition there was also General Wolff and myself. And as I strolled down the Sonneg Strasse from the Professor's house to the lake in the gentle evening sunshine the details of that dramatic meeting on another evening years before were still clear in my memory. Wolff and I were both striving desperately to persuade professional soldiers to make a break with their whole traditions for both political and humane reasons. In this we were supported by General Röttiger, von Vietinghoff's former Chief of Staff, and the Luftwaffe General von Pohl. Field Marshal Kesselring, now the Supreme Commander of all Germany's fast vanishing forces, was on a tour of inspection at the front and could not be reached. Field Marshal Alexander had just delivered what was practically an ultimatum, but our new Commander-in-Chief General Schultz was still unmoved by all the arguments we could bring forward.

At ten o'clock the ultimatum issued by Field Marshal Alexander expired. As the hour approached we still seemed no nearer a decision. The air in the deep bunker was so close as to be almost intolerable. As the hands of the clock came nearer and nearer ten, Wolff and I made a last, almost despairing attempt to convince at least the two army commanders. General Schultz was obviously hopeless. When we had finished we paused and looked round.

Then General Herr, commander of one of Germany's best armies quietly gave his Chief of Staff orders that the Tenth Army should cease fire on the following day at 14.00 hours. His example was followed by General Lemmelsen for the Fourteenth Army, General von Pohl for the Luftwaffe, Admiral Löwisch for the German naval units in Italy and General Wolff for the units under his command. There were no dramatics and no solemn words, and amidst the silence of the others Wolff then informed Field Marshal Alexander of what had been done.

A little later, at 11.15, the wireless announced that Adolf Hitler was dead. It was received almost with indifference. Most of those present had already taken their decision. All that was necessary now was the confirmation of the Supreme German Commander, Field Marshal Kesselring. I was present in Wolff's headquarters when the two men got into touch with each other at about midnight. I listened in to their conversation: the primarily military considerations of Kesselring balanced the primarily political considerations of Wolff. The conversation went on and on as each man expressed his human, military and political misgivings and convictions, and at 4.30 in the morning Field Marshal Kesselring, fully upholding his own military point of view, agreed that the capitulation recommended by Wolff for political reasons should go forward without hindrance.

The war in Italy was over.

And I had arrived at the Lake of Zürich. All I needed now to complete the day and crown my mood was to hear the evensong of the swans promised to me by my Swiss friends. I saw them glide up majestically looking like princes and princesses in a ballet, but it was only to snap at cream buns and other titbits held out to them by the be-ringed fingers of Zürich middle-class ladies. And instead of the swan song I had been expecting came harsh and raucous noises that sounded like: "More! More! More!"

The lights were going up now: in the lakeside hotels, on the pleasure yachts and the cabin cruisers, and on the huge Cadillacs waiting for the be-ringed ladies when they had finished feeding the swans. "More! More! More!" It all seemed very appropriate. Far more so than a swan song. That was a thing of the past. It didn't belong here.

I turned away from the lake and the lovely, greedy swans and made my way into the town. And of course, where could I have possibly landed that evening if not in Marry's Bar?

It had the reputation of being the representative place for foreign visitors. When I went inside I had the impression of entering the vestibule of an American army staff. The walls were covered with photographs of Anglo-American Generals all busily engaged in smiling from ear to ear and shaking hands with the proprietress of the place. They were everywhere, round the walls, at the back behind the bar, in the cloak-room, and above all the little tables. It made me wonder that the ceilings weren't painted with jet-bombers and atomic mushroom clouds. Montgomery, Eisenhower, Clark, Marshall—they were all there.

As I drank my Martini I couldn't help feeling that the Swiss really envied all other European countries their American forces of occupation. But at least America seemed to have conquered this particular Swiss bar, and to judge from all the photographs with the proprietress, fraternization had begun. An American juke-box began to play American music. It was too much. I finished my drink, paid for it and left. But just as I was taking my overcoat from the heavily made-up girl at the counter, the door opened and in walked a man I knew very well indeed, a big, powerful fellow in a well-cut suit of English cloth. It was Charlie Smith.

"Hullo, Eugenio!" he exclaimed when he spotted me. "What are you doing here? I thought you were in Lugano."

I had no time to answer and it would have taken too long anyhow.

"Not here," I said. "Let's go somewhere else."

I liked Charlie Smith. He was a man who had not only a good deal of charm but also millions to go with it. His great-grandfather had brewed beer in Dortmund, and very good beer it was. And when his grandfather took it to America the Americans thought so too. His father extended the business and Charlie himself already had an Anglo-Saxon name. They had all done very well with their Dortmund beer and Charlie could afford his little foibles. Apart from the beer he was interested in Ludwig II of Bavaria and Elizabeth of Austria, cocktails, and odd types like me—in my honour he called them all "Eugenios".

"Well, how are you?" he demanded cheerfully. "And what have you been up to? Why aren't you still in Lugano?"

"I got fed up with it in the end," I said. "And then there was a Communist type . . ."

And I told the whole story. He laughed heartily and slapped me on the back.

"Marvellous!" he exclaimed. "Can you beat it! We must have a drink on that."

We were outside the bar now.

"Not there," I said. "With all due respect I can't stand the faces of so many American heroes."

"Right you are," he said heartily. "Let's go to Dolder's then. I've booked a table there. Some oriental prince or other is coming and the place'll be packed."

"Right ho," I agreed. Oriental princes at least sounded a change from American army chiefs. We got into his car and drove off through the quiet streets of Zürich.

"Have you got a boiled shirt with you?" he asked.

I nodded.

"Couldn't come to Zürich without a boiled shirt, Charlie."

"Right. Get into it then."

He came back with me to my hotel and talked to me whilst I changed.

"I've got your two nephews with me," he said.

"What! You've brought Peter and Paul to Zürich?"

He grinned and nodded.

"Your cousin said they couldn't get used to modern society too early. After all, they're the future of Europe."

I made no comment.

"We ought to have a woman or two," I said.

Going down the stairs he informed me that he had made arrangements for that.

"We'll pick up Anitra and take her along," he said.

"Good God!" I exclaimed. Anitra was a woman I was constantly running into all over the world. She was a well-to-do Swiss who lived very comfortably from the proceeds of her father's factory. I couldn't think how Charlie had got hold of her, but there it was, and there was nothing to do about it now. And so with Charlie Smith, my two nephews Peter and Paul in sailor suits, and Anitra, whom Charlie had picked up somewhere or other, I walked through the revolving doors, across the large entrance hall, and down into the vast oval-shaped restaurant of the Grand Hotel Dolder, to which the promised presence of an Oriental prince had attracted the representatives of high society in large numbers.

Charlie inquired of the floor manager about the table he had booked, but the man shrugged his shoulders. No table had been reserved it appeared, and as all the tables were full we went back to the steps and stood there looking down at the guests. My nephews had gone off on their own. After dutifully kissing the hand of the ex-Queen of Roumania, they were now accepting ice and liqueurs from rich Swiss commoners. Charlie nodded to various friends. The floor manager had no time for the American beer baron so Charlie sat down on the steps and invited us to do the same, which we did. He then called the horrified head waiter and ordered champagne.

I sat on the soft tread of the steps with my shoes resting on the chromium rod which held the carpet in place. From where we were sitting it ran down the steps like a stream right out into the centre of the restaurant with its rather ornate Wilhelminian grandeur. At last the champagne arrived. The ex-Queen of Roumania rose and left the restaurant. The other guests sat below us at their tables, looking up from time to time in awe to us, as outsiders, who dared to challenge the accepted order and drink champagne on the steps, whilst they guarded their reserved places with as much devotion as the vestal virgins of ancient Rome had once guarded the holy fire.

Bright light fell onto the assembled guests from numerous crystal chandeliers and beyond the windows one could see the dark surface of the Lake of Zürich. I sat there and looked down at them, sipping my champagne reflectively. It was good champagne. They filled the place with their unctuous voices, their fat bellies and the glitter of their real and imitation diamonds. They were the profiteers of the last world-war—and the one before that. I had seen them all before. The first catastrophe had put millions into the pockets of their well-cut English suits. And after the second they were still there, still with their millions amidst the ruins of the Third Reich. No one could have detected even a single splash on their white shirt fronts which might have betrayed their business. The second catastrophe which had made them even richer was over now, but as they sat there eating their caviare, their oysters and their lobsters they were already thinking eagerly of a new source of diamonds for their women far, far away from the Lake of Zürich—Korea.

The excellent champagne bubbled in the long-stemmed glass in my hand, and my shoes rested on the chromium carpet rod on the steps of the Grand Hotel Dolder where we had deposited ourselves for want of a table amongst that illustrious gathering down below, where Chief Directors were served with telegrams on silver salvers as Tiberius had once been served with muraena fed on the flesh of slaves, where princesses nodded their heads condescendingly to devout film stars, and Swiss munitions makers sported their white-fronted shirts amongst their kind. Swiss armament shares had done better during the war, but never mind—new profits were beckoning there on the far away horizon where the flames of war were flickering again.

I knew what they were all thinking. Their thoughts are always so clearly visible on their faces, too clearly, too brutally. It is easy enough to see where the money comes from that buys their women diamonds and reserves tables for them at the exclusive Grand Hotel Dolder. They ought to conceal it better, but they know nothing of discretion.

I had had enough of the sight of them and I turned away. Beside me on the steps sat Mademoiselle, Fräulein, Signorina or Miss Anitra looking down with artificially bright eyes at the shining, diamond-studded oval of the restaurant Dolder. Despite her make-up she looked a little tired and a little worn, a little older too. I think at that moment she would sooner have been in her comfortable Swiss bed in her safe Swiss redoubt, nibbling a bar of Lindt chocolate and reading a thriller. But she couldn't stay there; Switzerland had to join in too. I felt a bit sorry for her, but only just a little bit. From Switzerland she had to traipse to Cannes and Biarritz, and from there to Kitzbühel and Salzburg, and back again. Lippizian mares and *Rosenkavalier*, slaloms and motor-car races, international film festivals and all-in wrestling didn't really interest her any more, and she would much sooner have stayed comfortably and peacefully in her native Zürich. But what could the poor girl do? Her social obligations drove her on relentlessly.

Sadism and masochism, homosexuality and perversity dominated the lives of this upper ten thousand. And in the deafening confusion of noise the old familiar sound of the Swiss cow-bells was lost. And that was not all that was lost, I thought. There was the native dance music of Honolulu, and the sound of the flutes of Korea. It all went under in the thunder of the guns—and every shell was worth a champagne evening to those assembled down below.

There I sat on the steps of the Grand Hotel Dolder and sipped champagne. Far above me were the servants' quarters and down below danced the cream of European high society with its decadent traditions, its profitable wars, its champagne and its narcotics.

I had once been a hero some said. When I prepared the capitulation of an army of eight hundred thousand men against the will of a daemonic lunatic. That could have cost me my life. Or when I saved men from the hands of their inhuman torturers. But that was past. Now I sat there without enough courage to go down into the restaurant and too cowardly to make my way, way up to where the servants lived. There I sat, a hero, a cowardly sort of hero, and sipped champagne on the steps of a luxury hotel, half way between the one and the other. I laughed.

Charlie looked at me.

"What are you laughing at, Eugenio?" he asked.

Then he saw that I was looking down into the restaurant.

"They like their liquor, don't they?" he said. "But there's a bit of a *Götterdammerung* atmosphere about, don't you think?"

"Just a bit," I replied. "Just a bit."